CRITICAL ACCLAIM FOR DAVID YEADON

"In *The Way of the Wanderer* David Yeadon captures the essential paradox (and wonder) of adventure travel: that passionately exploring the world is one of the best ways to get to know our own many 'selves.' Yeadon loves to travel, to explore, to observe, and has a real gift for making his own adventures enlighten and delight his readers."

—John Rasmus, editor-in-chief of *National Geographic Adventure*

"For those of us who see travel as an escape, David Yeadon offers a profound corrective. He regards it as a transcendent insight into the spirit of life itself, and this book is full of strange, moving and entertaining examples of his own responses, drawn from 25 years of wandering our mysterious globe."

—Jan Morris, author of *Fifty Years of Europe*

"*The Way of the Wanderer* is a magical gift. Yeadon's transformation through travel thrilled me and gave me hope for us all."

—Mikkel Aaland, author of *The Sword of Heaven*

"*The Back of Beyond* is a big, vigorous, hugely entertaining book of travels off-the-beaten path."

—Kirkus Reviews

"A very congenial traveling companion with the uncanny knack of blundering onto the real story of a place...."

—Tim Cahill, author of *Pass the Butterworms*

OTHER BOOKS BY DAVID YEADON

The Back of Beyond: Travels to the Wild Places of the Earth
Backroad Journeys of the West Coast State
Backroad Journeys of Southern Europe
Secluded Islands of the Atlantic Coast
Hidden Corners of New England
New York's Best Places

The Way of the Wanderer

The Way of the Wanderer

Discover Your
True Self
through Travel

WRITTEN AND ILLUSTRATED
BY DAVID YEADON

TRAVELERS' TALES
SAN FRANCISCO

Travelers' Tales and Travelers' Tales Guides are trademarks of Travelers' Tales, Inc., 330 Townsend Street, Suite 208, San Francisco, California 94107. www.travelerstales.com

Cover Design: Michele Wetherbee
Interior Design: Melanie Haage
Cover Illustration: David Yeadon
Illustrations: David Yeadon
Page Layout: Melanie Haage, using the fonts Sabon and Charme

Distributed by Publishers Group West, 1700 Fourth Street, Berkeley, California 94710.

Library of Congress Cataloging-in-Publication Data
Yeadon, David.
    The way of the wanderer : discover your true self through travel / written and illustrated by David Yeadon.—1st ed.
        p.   cm.
    ISBN 1-885211-60-0
    1. Yeadon, David—Journeys. 2. Voyages and travels.
    3. Self-realization. I. Title.

G465 .Y43 2001
910.4—dc21   00-053682

First Edition
Printed in the United States of America
10 9 8 7 6 5 4 3 2 1

for
ANNE
my wife, my partner, my friend
and very definitely...
one of my best me-s

TABLE OF CONTENTS

We live but a fraction of our life.
Why do we not let in the flood, raise the gates,
and set all our wheels in motion?

—HENRY DAVID THOREAU

Everyone with a taste for adventure has felt the impulse to travel to remote and strange destinations where life might lose all trace of gray banality. Caught in a daily regimen of work and survival, many of us long for the exotic and the magical where new vistas may suddenly unfold before our awe-filled gaze. But what lies at the root of this impulse that compels us to shake off the dusty familiarity of well-trodden streets and head beyond the beyond?

David Yeadon has answered that inner call to adventure far more than most, and can look back on a lifetime of wandering the planet—from the foggy moorlands of his native England to the deepest jungles of South America and the silent, empty beaches of forgotten tropical islands. Decades of rich experience in many of the world's most beautiful places, countless nights alone under strange skies in wild lands, have taught him much about what it is that drives us from our comfortable beds and easy routines to face danger, loneliness, miserable cold, or suffocating heat.

This is a travel book with a difference; for *The Way of the Wanderer* is ultimately the quest for self-knowledge, the eternal journey toward deeper insight into our true nature. Most travelers today may appear on the surface to be just another bunch of men and women with backpacks and dreams of freedom. But underneath there are echoes of ancient Taoist sages and Zen priests, wandering cloud-hidden among the herbs and flowers of silent hills, intent on unlocking wisdom and awareness. By traveling to distant parts of the world we discover hitherto unsuspected parts of our self, or perhaps it is better to say that we find new selves. The traveler who is honest enough with himself about the highs and lows, the fears and ecstasies of journeying through unknown landscapes is equipped to find new treasures within his own psyche. These are the permanent gifts with which he returns home, and which enrich him long after once vivid experiences have turned to dim memories.

Yet this is not simply a book of self-discovery. It is a work filled with a gifted writer's capacity to evoke the smells, colors, noises, and elemental power of a vast range of amazing locations. Trudging with the author along a windswept Lakeland ridge, learning the secrets of flora and fauna from the Aboriginal people of Australia's desert Outback, stumbling and sliding up the bizarre rock pillars of Venezuelan Amazonia, tasting near-death among the surging ocean waves, we are gripped by the storyteller's art. This is a book that hugely enriches the reader's imagination. It leaves an impression of an enormously full life packed with the kind of intense and soulful experiences that most people would feel fortunate to know only once or twice.

Of course, such a life does not happen by accident—it is a consequence of courageous decisions at moments of destiny when a fork in life's road offers a choice between the comfort of familiarity or the risks of the unknown. David Yeadon has been blessed with a brave capacity to follow his heart, relax in the fullness of the present moment, and trust what fate may bring if it is met with confidence and openness to authentic human contact. In these pages we see clearly those moments, on a narrow bridge near the Caspian Sea or in a remote village in the Canary Islands, where he took his stand for freedom and self-knowledge.

It is the wealth of selves familiar to the author that enables him to connect so deeply with so many different kinds of people and elicit from them nuggets of unexpected wisdom. The cheery pub landlord at the end of a 190-mile trek, the enigmatic and mysteriously enlightened Caribbean boatman, the scarred Himalayan kayaker filled with knowledge of life at the edge, all reveal sudden depths of humanity. They all point to one of the greatest realizations: that beyond the clutter and bustle of hectic, often confused lives, "our world remains a thing of mystery, silence and secrets."

It is the attempt to discover these secrets that forms the unspoken agenda in each of these tales. For the awakened traveler, every journey is a "double exploration" of both outer and inner worlds, and the simple adventure of travel has the potential to become a kind of natural spiritual path, available to all wanderers regardless of creed or belief system. This book is a distillation of a lifetime's travel and exploration and is suffused with the kind of warmth and grace that come from decades devoted to following one's dreams, regardless of the practical consequences. I can think of few works that have the capacity to transport the reader to such varied and exotic locales with such vividness and immediacy. These pictures of distant lands, whether drawn with words or pencil, leave the reader with a wonderfully nourishing sense of the spectacular abundance, variety and beauty of our planet, and the wisdom and simple humanity of its inhabitants. Eventually, we come to suspect that it is this deep and full affirmation of life that is itself the inner fruit of these marvelously rendered outer journeys.

—Ralph White

Ralph White is editor of Lapis *magazine and co-founder of the New York Open Center.*

The Ramblings of a "Lost Worlds" Explorer

*"The wanderer is overcome by the joy of
existence so that he can only laugh."*
—*Tibetan Dhyani Buddha*

The wandering Earth Gypsy in me has long been a restless and
driven fellow inspired in part, I guess, by the Buddha quote above
(it's true—I do tend to laugh a lot) and by those timeless and tantalizing lines of John Donne:

> To live in one land is captivitie,
> To runne all countries—a wild roguerie!

Fortunately I've managed to tame and focus my gypsy a little
by becoming a writer and illustrator of adventure travel books.
And in these books, over the years I've become increasingly
accustomed to using unfamiliar and exotic places—"lost
worlds" if you will—as a metaphor for self-exploration and the

discovery of inner lost worlds. So join me briefly in one of my earlier experiences:

I am on an island. An ocean of sloppy, slow-moving wavelets, shimmering in a heat mist; a fringe of low, bent palms offering welcome shade and a beach of the most beautiful pink sand I've ever seen anywhere in the world—a magnificent slowly-curving strand of talcum-softness stretching into hazy infinities in both directions. Untouched, unbroken, unspoiled by any sign of human intrusion. No buildings, no boats, no people, no nothing. Just this perfect place—this tiny island—this little lost world set in a turquoise ocean under a dome of blue sky. And it's all mine!

I realize here, once again, that the magic of journeys and explorations is not to be found merely in the external adventures and discoveries—wonderful and terrifying though they are—but in the worlds that such experiences lead us to find within ourselves. Those "other spaces" in the spirit that beckon and tantalize us all, but in which we may spend too little time.

When I allow my eyes to really see, freed from the filters of the mind, I'm amazed at how much I don't see most days. In the mystery and silence of this evening I'm tingling. Time doesn't really exist anymore. My watch is stowed deep in the backpack and my body begins to respond to its own rhythms. Rhythms of which I'm too often unaware.

We have to be alone to touch our inner selves. And if we cannot touch ourselves, how can we ever truly touch anyone else?

A question comes: "Who are you going to be today?" And then a thought, which I scribble in a sea-stained notepad:

> Ah!
> to have no rigid goals and plans
> except to be
> all the am-s, I am.

And to celebrate too
all the you-s
in
you.

That was all a few years back, but I still have the yellowed note today, tacked to the wall above my desk. When I first wrote it I wasn't too sure what it meant, but I kept it anyway and left my lovely, lonely island after days of slow, mind-evolving, beach-wandering and moved on to Australia.

Things then became a little clearer while drowning.

It was my near-death experience #3 (in twenty-five years of adventure travel writing, I have had a total of five, and that is just about right) and the fickle riptides and wave-crests of the Western Australian ocean were whirlpooling me down for the third and final time. I was experiencing a very odd range of emotions, as if a plethora of different people were inside me fighting for attention while I was very preoccupied with the process of drowning. One was a dour doomsayer convinced that death was nigh and flailing about in a panic-stricken state trying to grab a last breath before the final wet darkness; the second was a somewhat indifferent projectionist playing a crazed film collage of mostly forgotten head-clips of random, and often poignant, life events as the currents pulled me down; the third was the good old writer-journalist—I knew him pretty well—thinking what a great tale this would make if only he could keep notes—and stay alive, of course; then a fourth, far less known to me, that in the midst of the chaos and confusion brought enormous, quiet calm with an illuminating certainty that seemed to say, "There's so much more to come, so many things you've never dreamed of...."

Needless to say, I survived (thanks to the timely action of a true-blue, *Baywatch*-built, good-on-yer-mate Aussie) and when the nightmarish strangeness of it all had diminished I was left with one clear realization—that there seemed to be a heck of a lot of people living inside me and it was time I met more of them and let them out into the world for a romp. Suddenly that little scribbled island note-to-myself took on fresh significance.

To be honest, the idea of the "multi-me" was not altogether new. Travel writing has taken me to some pretty odd places around the globe and put me in situations that, looking back, make me wonder incredulously at my naiveté, stupidity, and blatant bombast in the face of seemingly doom-laden situations. As each crazy adventure was surmounted by even crazier escapades, I'd gain fleeting glimpses of other me-s— unfamiliar characters who emerged unexpectedly to perceive something, say something, or perform some act completely out of character, and then vanish again into what I thought was the "real" me. On these occasions the consistent, unified, "centered being" I assumed myself to be just kind of stood there watching in amazement and occasionally amusement. Who, I would wonder, was that? And who, for that matter, am "I"?

Dismissing chronic schizophrenia as something that did not appear to run in the family, I began observing some of these "other me-s" in more detail. At first it was like pursuing the tail end of dreams—you remember the emotive force but the rich shadowy details fade fast. But over time, a few of them became more familiar, even good friends, and I found they had much to say, much to teach that—given a more traditional life—I might well have ignored.

T. S. Eliot was right: "Each venture is a new beginning." To which I would add—and a "new being," a new range of insights and discoveries of the self, or rather, other facets or manifestations of this complex oddity we so curiously call *the* self. We all find our own unique ways of exploring these inner-selves. We use the familiar stimulants of meditation, mystic meanderings, music, philosophical-theosophical studies, "altered state" devices in whatever combination seems to work best. For some reason I chose travel as my stimulant of choice and catalyst of inner explorations. In my earlier life I was a city planner in England and later in various other parts of the world, and though I say it myself, I was a pretty good "urban designer"— mildly ambitious, with no complaints at all about inflated salaries, generous expense accounts, company cars and all the beguiling enticements of ladder-climbing professional success.

And so it came as much as a surprise to me as to my colleagues when I suddenly gave it all up at the ripe age of thirty. I said I intended to take a three-month sabbatical but apparently I lied. So far it's been a twenty-five-year hiatus and— given a reasonable chance of modest mortality—it'll stretch on another twenty-five. Maybe it was that delightful line from Agassiz that started it all: "I cannot afford to waste my time making money," or Joseph Campbell's releasing reminder: "Trust your bliss—walk on!"

As I grew more aware of the "multi-me" concept, I found I was not alone. Joseph Campbell again:

> When we travel we meet ourselves in other guises...by exploring ourselves in many forms of humanity we travel lifetimes in the course of an instant.

And Robert Jay Lifton in his intriguing book, *The Protean Self*:

> We are all multiple from the start...we are by nature multi-minded...we are fluid and many-sided...evolving a self of many possibilities.

A friend of mine who has experienced a series of death-defying illnesses and other catastrophes recently returned to life outrageously reinvigorated and told me with an idiot grin, "Dying's not the risk—that's the sure thing. The risk is not living."

So—for life's sake—let's live! It's a risk we avoid at our peril, for why would anyone ignore or discard the one truly free gift we have? And travel has nothing to do with it really. Others have "taken the risk" in far less arduous ways of inner-journeying than my haphazard ramblings around the globe. Even I find the constant need for movement and new experiences a little mellowed now. The inner journeys seem to continue quite happily at my desk, by the lake, in the garden, cooking, rambling the rutted back roads a few miles from home, or while performing the most mundane of tasks. My me-s emerge and move more freely now and as I meet and embrace each new persona (nuance, facet—call them what you will), I find inevitably that I naturally embrace far more readily the multihued dimensions of other people I meet or new situations in which I find my-selves.

So let me summarize the key ideas behind this book:

We are, each one of us, shards, fragments, holograms of the Creator and/or (depending on how tolerant you are of single-creator concepts) the Creative Wholeness of the universe.

Each one of us, it thus follows, is extravagantly and exuberantly multi-dimensional, multi-faceted, multi-talented, and multi-selved.

However (and it's a rather significant "however"), for reasons only fear, cynicism, or ignorance can explain, most of us have been intentionally indoctrinated, programmed, and very often effectively convinced that we can and should use only as modest a number of these multi-selves as possible. This, we are told, is because of their insidious tendency to create a permanent state of personal experimentation which can obviously lead to such dire consequences as irrational joy, inconsistency, restlessness, unpredictability, and can stimulate excessive urges of a highly erratic—even ecstatic—nature, which, in turn, may be disconcerting and unsettling to personal and family lives and society in general—and downright spiritually anarchistic in some instances.

The problem with all this erroneous programming is that, for reasons we often find convenient to ignore, we tend to forget that the single driving force behind human evolution and the only thing that makes our little world tick and evolve is (dare I say that much-misused word) L-O-V-E. Substitute more acceptable terms such as mutual empathy, tolerance, and understanding if you wish—anything that encourages us to listen to and learn from one another and see others in our-selves and vice versa.

Once we recognize the idea—the reality—that we do, each single one of us, "contain multitudes" (Walt Whitman's words), then it follows that we might naturally be meant to mutually celebrate the release of our individual multitudes and, as a species, learn to evolve together more effectively—and enjoyably—through mutual empathy and support. Obviously, the more you see and celebrate the kaleidoscopic richness in your own spirit, the more you're able and willing to celebrate the kaleidoscopic array of other human spirits and, for that matter, our species as a whole.

☞

As I said before, I chose travel as my conduit to these multi-selves. Real travel. Personal travel. Adventure and exploration. Endless. No finales, only preludes. The kind of travel that tingles and reverberates and resonates and sends symphonies of enlightenment and transformation rippling through our souls. The kind of travel that requires not so much exotic, distant places (it's amazing how much adventure you can enjoy close to home) but rather some willingness on the part of the traveler to let go, to seek serendipity and celebrate uncertainty, vulnerability, the thrills of fresh discoveries, and the riches of inner journeys that recognize that their ultimate destination is ourselves.

And this door is open to you. To each and every one of us.

So, there it is. This book is a clarion call to us all to learn to live and travel through life in a true Renaissance Spirit. You'll likely meet an amazing array of characters inside yourself, characters you had no idea existed. And that will merely be the beginning of the greatest adventure of all—the celebration of life—your whole multi-self life—and thus the lives of our whole human miracle.

Now, if chords have been struck in your head, heart, or soul, then read on, and keep traveling and celebrating the ongoing rebirthing of all your-selves.

May you enjoy all your journeys.

—DAVID YEADON
Kyushu, Japan

*Walk down
as many roads
as possible.*

—PHIL COUSINEAU

Almost Gone #1
The Bridge—
Where All the
Adventures Began

In which I glimpse one of life's greatest mysteries.

I think I travel because I'm alive. And I don't mean that to sound glib. I mean that I really should be dead. A part of me still thinks that maybe I did die years ago when I was an ambitious urban planner working in Iran on the future master plan for the city of Tehran, and that someone else, another me, in fact, quite a generous array of me-s—took over my body and mind and have been living here happily ever since.

It's a short story, but still a disconcerting one. Even as I write it now I feel an odd tremor through my fingers.

My wife Anne and I were high up in the Elburz Mountains of Iran. This dramatic range acts as a 14,000-foot wall separating Tehran and the desert from the lush jungled hills bordering the Caspian Sea. We'd had a few lazy days of meandering, trying to learn a little more about this anomalous country and its long history. We were returning back over the mountains on the "old road," a narrow unpaved trail that promised more adventure than the carefully graded curves and tunnels of the new road a couple of hundred miles to the west. Everything was going fine. There was no traffic and we felt very much at peace among the peaks and high valleys.

We were descending a steep pass, the road curling and twisting through a broken stretch of country. Around a sharp bend we approached a one-lane bridge with no retaining wall on either side—just a vertical drop of 300 feet or so into a shadowy ravine. A dramatic place. Then suddenly, with no warning, an enormous Mack truck came barreling across the bridge from the other side spewing rocks and dust. He, like us, assumed he had the road to himself and was trying to gain acceleration for the long climb up the pass. By this time we were actually on the bridge, which seemed hardly wide enough for one car, let alone two vehicles heading straight for each other. We realized he couldn't possibly brake without careening off the bridge. We also knew the same applied to us, and there wasn't time to stop anyway. But I did brake. I didn't know what else to do. And—like watching a slow-motion film—we could see our car skidding sideways right toward the wall-less edge of the bridge, and the ravine. We both closed our eyes and I remember two silly things quite distinctly: a beautiful color of bright purple inside my closed eyelids, and feeling a strip of torn leather on the steering wheel and wondering why I'd never repaired it. We were still skidding; I could hear the gravel hissing under the sliding tires. We waited, eyes still closed, for the collision with the truck or for the fall into the ravine—or both. We were absolutely calm. No screams. Just acceptance.

What seemed like minutes later, but can only have been a second or two, we opened our eyes to find ourselves moving very slowly forward, down the center of the bridge. The car seemed to be driving itself. We pulled to a stop and looked behind us. There was no truck. No dust. We got out of the car and listened. There was no sound—no indication that the truck had ever been there at all. We were absolutely calm; no fear, no shaking, no aftereffects of shock. We just kept looking around and then looked at each other. We even looked over the bridge to see if the truck had tumbled into the ravine. Nothing.

We got back into the car and drove on. We didn't speak for a long time. Then Anne said: "That did happen, didn't it?"

"It happened" was all I could think to say. Though what had actually happened we couldn't understand. All we knew was that something very strange had taken place, and we were still alive. And then we were weeping. Great big sobs. And then laughing, and then very quiet for most of the journey back to Tehran.

*

Many people experience some climactic event that makes a radical change in their lives. Well, this was ours. We still don't know what happened; we don't know if we "lost" our old selves and somehow emerged unscathed and "new"; and we don't know how we survived when it was obvious even now, having written it all down, I'm none the wiser. Wiser, that is, about the event itself. But we both became far wiser in other ways that completely transformed our lives.

We began to understand with greater clarity the fragility and wonder of life itself; we knew from that moment on we would try to live our lives to the fullest, doing what we felt, deep down, we should be doing, no longer putting things off until we had accumulated enough cash or confidence, or security, or whatever it takes, to feel "free." We found our freedom on that bridge. And we needed for nothing after that. Even though there were difficult years in material and other ways, we never had any doubts about what we were doing with our lives. It didn't always make sense, particularly to others. But somehow that singular experience bored a hole into our souls and certainty flowed out and has just kept on flowing.

And it is that sense of certainty that has acted as a catalyst for all our ongoing adventures and explorations around the globe which, over the years (a lot of years!) has revealed so much to us of the magic and mystery of our earth and the peoples who inhabit it.

And, as we explored outwardly so we inevitably explored inwardly—deeper and deeper, revealing hosts of newly discovered selves we have been getting to know ever since.

If you haven't experienced that "climactic event," look for small signs and listen to your inner voice. That "certainty" about your true path is there, like the oak tree in the acorn.

I would rather live in a world where my life is surrounded by mystery than live in a world so small my mind would comprehend it.
—PASTOR HARRY EMERSON FOSDICK

The Gate—
My Very First
Exploration

*At any age, a universe of possibilities lies just
outside your door.*

I left home at the age of four.

Don't get me wrong. I loved my parents, our cat Prudence, my bedroom, my toys, and my mum's Yorkshire pudding on Sundays. I even loved my baby sister. Sometimes.

But someone had left the gate out of the garden onto the street unlocked and—I could just reach the latch....

And so I left home.

And, honestly, to this very day, I can still remember that delicious, almost-erotic frisson that moved up and down my spine like electricity and made me feel ten feet high and as

brave as a bull. So off I went, a little tentatively at first, keeping close to the small brick walls and neatly cropped privet hedges that lined our street and well away from the road that I'd been told constantly was "very, very dangerous." But after a while I got cocky. I even dipped into the gutter to pick up a stick that looked like a sword. And then, when my courage was really up, I actually crossed the street into a shadowy alley that I'd seen before from my father's car but never thought I'd have the chance to explore all by myself. So it was down the alley, along by the stores on Main Street, then down by the pond, and then near the factory that made bicycles—I felt I'd traveled miles and miles—until a very hawkish lady with a hair bun, a scratchy tweed coat, a purple spotty nose, and a way of talking that made her sound like an angry parrot, decided that I was "lost." (Lost indeed! I was doing just fine.) She said I needed to be taken to the local police station and kept there "until we find your irresponsible parents—fancy letting you out all by yourself, you could have been..." etc., etc. You know the stuff. I didn't at the time of course.
It was all new to me.

But—and now I come to the crux of the whole adventure —precisely which "me" shouldn't have been "let out" was unclear because this little adventure revealed for the very first time just how many new me-s were lurking about in the me I thought I knew and recognized every day.

For example, there was the *Coward*-me who cringed and cried and crept like a scared mouse up the alley trailed by a snarling terrier with yellow teeth that looked as large as a lion...

...and then came:

the me that suddenly popped out and realized I had a stick (sword) in my hand and that the terrier had to be punished with a sharp whack for his arrogant bad temper (he was and he ran like hell and my *Warrior*-me felt absolutely magnificent).

the *Gourmet*-me. Not satisfied with finding a recently abandoned ice cream with some very pink, strawberry ice cream still left intact, I slurped away with gay abandon and even added the petals of some miniature roses I plucked from a garden because they smelled so nice.

the *Shy*-me who rarely talked to anyone outside the immediate family suddenly found himself reborn as the *Conversationalist* as I strolled nonchalantly down Main Street pausing to say hello to a postman, a young boy twice my age (he liked me and gave me a "conker" nut, which we used in those days in a popular string game), a butcher painting his daily offerings in whitewash on his store window, and what I thought was a very friendly old lady in a fur coat that made her look like a huge bear, but who turned out to be not so friendly and asked the lady with the parrot voice to "do something with him."

And at least a dozen other me-s including the *Thief*—I pinched a "licorice-allsort" from a tray near the counter of a candy store—the lady behind the counter saw me do it but she just smiled and gave me another one!; the *Trickster*—I almost escaped from the parrot-voice pretending I had to go to the bathroom. Unfortunately, she couldn't find one; the *Con Artist*—I managed to wangle sixpence from a fat man with a big mustache by poking my eyes and making them water and saying I'd lost my money my mum had given me to buy bread; the *Good Samaritan* (twice)—by helping a greengrocer retrieve a spilled box of oranges from the sidewalk (without pocketing one) and by giving my newly gained sixpence to a little girl who looked even sadder than I looked (maybe she was a *Con Artist* too), and on and on....

So by the time I was delivered intact back home, safely behind the gate with a brand new lock on it and sitting on the knee of my very sheepish-looking father who apparently had created all the commotion by a little carelessness, I reckon I'd found a couple dozen fresh permutations of me—new people I'd never really been aware of before—contradictory, multi-faceted, good-bad, dumb-bright—the lot.

And then, when I started to tell my eventually mollified family about all my adventures, I found them listening with rapt attention, laughing in all the right places, asking for more, and hugging me and telling me what a wonderful storyteller I was (first emergence of the *Raconteur* here) and how,

one day I might even grow up to be a WRITER!

(And believe me, it was downhill all the way after that suggestion became embedded in a very spritely young psyche.)

Do not be satisfied with the stories that come before you; unfold your own myths.
    —RUMI

The Island — Rediscovering the Gift of Solitude

Try taking just yourself along for company—
it's the best way to find your path.

I recently did something that all of us fantasize about every once in a while. I sailed out with a local fisherman (Frigate Bird Sam they called him—a real barnacled, broad-grinned kind of mariner—and there's a letter of thanks to him at the end of this tale) to a virtually deserted Caribbean island graced with seemingly soft coral-pink sand and gave myself a few days of total solitude just to see what would happen, and it turned out to be a rather illuminating experience.

I have nowhere special to go, nothing to do. I don't even have to listen to my restless mind, if I can persuade it to switch off for a while and become part of this beautiful place.

"Be patient," I tell myself.

And slowly, slowly as a rising tide, the calm comes.

At one point, meandering across the endless sands, letting the grains tickle my toes, I look down on my mind as if floating over a familiar turbulent landscape. And what clutter I see there—what a jumbled topography of fears and feelings and disjointed, shadowy memories. Like an attic into which I throw things haphazardly, promising myself the pleasures of sorting it all out one day into neat piles and boxes. I've noticed I do that with my studio back home—letting it become a chaotic mess of papers and drawings and slide boxes and half-finished writings and notes to myself and broken pencils and unread magazines. And then—suddenly—in a whirl of organizing glee, I file, fold, pack, stack, and rack all the clutter into neatly labeled packages, sweep the floors, clean the windows, wash fingerprints and coffee stains and cigar ash from my desk. And it's new again. A model studio, almost fit to be photographed for the glossy "house" magazines. Ah. If only minds could be tidied up so neatly and so quickly.

But there again, unlike my studio, which is the only working space I have, my head has other spaces I can enter, spaces beyond the finite mind, that are far less cluttered. A little cobwebby perhaps from underuse, but lean and roomy and fresh. Spaces to dream in; spaces in which to experience new sensations and see new patterns of understanding; spaces to explore, as seemingly infinite as this beach and the ocean that skitters and dances and plays across its pinkness.

I realize once again that the magic of "lost world" exploration is not to be found merely in wonderful and exotic adventures but in the lost worlds revealed to us deep within ourselves—infinitely rich worlds of wonder, wisdom, and human "wholeness."

⁂

The sun is sinking now, easing down through the darkening blues into brilliant layers of scarlet, crimson, and old gold. And here I am. On the quietest, most peaceful place of all. Alone. Enjoying Robinson Crusoe fantasies and writing snippets of thoughts to myself as the sunset gilds the trunks of the leaning palm trees and sends shimmers of gold threading across the frothy tops of lazy waves.

Lying quietly here, with no thoughts except this one.

I feel renewed in some way, excited by the smallest details which I'm seeing as if for the first time—a flash of light on the crystalline surfaces of sand grains; the purposeful, determined movements of a tiny crab, hardly bigger than a dime, scurrying along the edges of the sloppy surf; the slow circle patterns traced in the sky hundreds of feet above me by five frigate birds, wings outstretched but unmoving, merely floating on the spirals. I'm here, emptied, waiting to be filled again.

I strip off everything and stroll into the ocean, letting the water lick around my ankles. I hear the suck of surf, the gentle grasp of the tide, the rumble of pebbles moving in the deeper places, and sense the slow rounding down of everything.

I walk in until the sea reaches my navel and then turn to lie on my back, letting the warm water hold me, moving me slowly into the shore, then easing me out again. Solitude seems so natural now. Life welcomes the void and fills me—with little secrets.

Much later I find a bowl of soft sand between two palms. I spread out my groundsheet, spray myself against an expected onslaught of mosquitoes that never comes, and light a small fire of dead palm fronds and broken branches dragged from the scrub behind the beach. I plan a dinner from a handful of dehydrated food packages and then realize I'm not hungry. How about a fish? About time you tried out that little boy scout box with the nylon line and the brightly colored float. But somehow the idea of actually killing something and eating it doesn't appeal. A handful of dried fruits and raisins is fine.

And then something very odd. A sudden change of mood. I feel very alone. Even vulnerable. A shiver of fear starts in my neck and jiggers all the way to my toes. Fear of what? I can't pin it down. I just have this need for company. For some familiar sound or voice. Even a radio...that's it. My trusty little shortwave radio. My dependable friend that keeps me in touch with the world in the remotest of places. I reach out for my backpack and feel around in the dim light for its familiar form. Out it comes, earphone and all. Switch it on. It's already switched on. And there's no little red light to tell me I'm tuned in to the BBC World Service, or Radio Moscow, or Voice of America—or even Radio Cuba. Nothing at all. Just a useless black plastic box with two burnt-out batteries and no replacements. Well, I didn't know I was going to go wandering off like this. If I'd known I was going to do this dumb Robinson Crusoe thing I'd have brought all kinds of stuff—my tiny tape player, more food, a flashlight, books.

I scribble depressing thoughts in my notebook: A loneliness creeps in with the dusk, lowering the ceiling of thoughts, closing off feelings, edging out the adventure.

A voice inside niggles. "So now you're really on your own, mate!" My mind whirls around like a caged monkey, trying to find a way to subdue this surge of loneliness and these odd fears. It's crazy. There I was, an hour or so ago, blissfully floating in the ocean, writing little mellow thoughts to myself, absorbed in the silence and stillness of this place. And now here I am, struggling like a straightjacketed madman, desperately seeking noise and distraction, unable to return to those calm, tranquil spaces in my head.

It's all so ridiculous. This earth-wanderer, explorer of wild places, panicked because his stupid shortwave radio won't work and scared by the sounds and rustling movements in the scrub behind him.

"There's something in there!" that damnable little voice shrieks inside my skull.

But what? I'd heard there were no snakes here—at least none that are dangerous. Maybe a few wild pigs, but most of those were supposed to be way off on the other side of the island around by the caves and clefts of the limestone "highlands." So what the hell is moving back there?

I turn to stare into the thick scrub. In the light of the dying fire I can see nothing except dark shadows.

Forget it, I tell myself. Enjoy the last of the light, faintly pink behind the black silhouettes of the far islands. Get your head back to where it was before. Have a drink of rum. Write another one of those scribbles to yourself. Stop thinking! Just enjoy being here.

But I am right.

There *is* something behind me. I can hear it moving closer now, coming through the scrub toward me. The faint crack of a twig; a rattling of dry leaves. Something is there. I sit absolutely motionless. Whatever it is may not have seen me. And I can escape easily. A fast trot into the sea—even a quick scamper up one of the palm trees. I'm safe.

And the deer obviously thinks so too.

It steps daintily out of the bushes a few yards to my left, lifting small feet in a tiptoe motion, easing across the spikey grasses between the palms and coming to stand on the cusp of the beach where the sand slopes down into the barely moving wavelets.

It seems a very small deer, hardly more than hip-height. Maybe a young fawn. And barely distinguishable from the shadows in the last glimmers of dusk. Except for the eyes. Bright, full, and unblinking. Staring straight at me. We both remain absolutely still. Its tail and ears are erect. I don't sense any fear in the creature. Perhaps a little caution, but mostly curiosity. It takes a couple of steps towards me, shaking each of its front legs as it walks and then pauses and lowers its head, maybe as a way of seeing me better. Maybe even a gesture of acknowledgment. I've never been so close to a deer before except in a zoo and I breathe as quietly as I can. I know little about these animals although I've always loved the gracefulness of their movements.

The deer raises its head again and allows its tail to drop. Its eyes are still fixed on mine. Such calm eyes. Beguiling.

And then it's gone. A shake of the head, a flick of the tail, and gentle dainty retreat into the dark scrub behind the palms.

I sit for a long time in silence, letting the joy-waves ride up and down my body. I don't need the radio now. I don't need company, or distractions. All those elusive fears, the loneliness, are gone.

For tonight at least, I just need me.

☙

Time doesn't really exist anymore. My watch is stowed deep in the backpack and my body begins to respond to its own rhythms. Rhythms of which I'm too often unaware. I sleep when I'm sleepy or when it's too hot to walk out on the open beach. I boil a packet of beef stroganoff for breakfast because I suddenly feel like eating beef Stroganoff. Half-heartedly I try fishing in the shallows with the line and float and a bit of leftover beef as bait. But I think even the fish can sense I'm not really trying. And it's too hot anyway. They're doubtless off in deeper, cooler places doing whatever fish do down there in the heat of the day.

I scribble more "thoughts-to-myself" as I stroll through the surf in the early evening. And the beach just goes on and on—endlessly arcing away in both directions, mile after mile of soft pink sand unmarked by footprints or anything else that suggests the island has ever seen a human here before.

"It's all mine."

That one thought keeps dancing through my head like a woodland sprite. Rarely, if ever, have I felt so free and unencumbered by plans or projects or fears or uncertainties. I have no guides to worry about or, as is more usually the case, to worry about me. I have no one to meet, nothing to say, nothing even to think, if I don't feel like thinking.

And that's what I'm enjoying most. The lack of thinking. For much of the time my mind is content to see without looking, to feel without analyzing. Just to be. To walk softly in the glimmering light...and disappear!

I am learning to expect nothing—to expect no expectations. So what comes? Lovely surprises, of course, all the time. The perfection of a shell in all its whirling wonder; the shapes in a piece of driftwood—two horses, a hand, a mountain landscape in miniature, a breast pertly nippled; the incredible life in a dead vine still clutching, strangling, a withered tree trunk. So many moments in a single moment!

Letting go, flowing with the flow of things and, for a single second, being infinite.

I find myself walking on tiptoe even in the soft sand so as not to bruise that special silence before dusk, before the noises in the bushes and the cool evening breezes that make the palm fronds go *clacker-clacker-clacker*.

And after all this today, more surprises tomorrow.
I've hardly begun.

✐

Because I've slept during the day I feel like walking at night under a creamy half-moon and a canopy festooned with star patterns. The beach is a silver strip, edged by a sparkling sea that hardly moves at all. In the quietness of this night I meet myself again and rediscover so many things I'd forgotten.

Finally sleep eases in so I spread out the groundsheet, bunch up the backpack as a pillow and drift off with a final thought for the day: I hope all this never ends; I hope I never arrive.

✐

On the third day—I think it's the third day anyway— there's a storm, a real humdinger.

Out in the west, among the silhouetted islands, the sky is clear and bright. But in the other direction it's as black as a mineshaft. I don't think I've ever seen a sky as black anywhere. The wind, a few minutes ago nothing more than a pleasant trade breeze, bashes into the palms like a prizefighter going for a knockout in the first round. The surf itself turns black, showing its true colors, discarding the simpering turquoises and royal blues, throwing off its limpid lappings on the shore and gathering muscle by the minute. The gentle chitter of pebbles in the undertow is replaced by an ominous grinding and pounding as coral boulders, deeper down, begin to move against one another. The sea seethes up the pink beach, now turning blood red as the first egg-sized splatters of rain hit, sending up sprays of fine silica. It races far higher up the sand than before, pauses as if in frustration that it has failed to reach the tree line, and then tears back down the slope of the beach to consolidate itself in even higher, blacker waves that rise up like ancient battered walls to surge forward once again.

This is the ocean I love. This is when you feel its strength and majesty—when you know it can destroy boats, men, houses, even whole communities, in the power of its latent spirit. You become too beguiled and entranced by its apparent docility; you forget how oceans can shape and meld whole continents; you ignore its primeval force and nature.

But not now!

I find a hollow away from the gesticulating palms and flying fronds, up close to the sturdy thick scrub. And I watch as the rain thrashes the grasses, breaking them and pounding them into the soft earth. I don't think I'd like to be a palm tree in this storm. They've learned the benefits of flexibility—they sway and bend and throw their fronds high like the outstretched gesticulating arms of Arab women at a wake—but each storm saps their strength, weakens their roots, stretches their fibrous trunks to breaking point, and leaves them more vulnerable to the next onslaught. I've seen dozens of them on my walk, dead and discarded like driftwood, half buried in sand, their broken roots still screaming at the air—eternal reminders of battles fought and lost in the seething, scathing tumult of hurricanes.

I am lost in the power of the storm. Soaked, shivering (the wind is actually cold), and shocked by the suddenness of it all, I give myself up to its roar and its rage.

On and on, blacker and blacker, louder and louder. Maybe this really is a hurricane. With my radio out of action I've heard no warnings. My one hope is that Sam is comfortable and safe at home and not out on the ocean in this maelstrom. The growling and grinding from the surf is almost animal-like now. A fierce, teeth-tingling sound. Waves hit the shore like mortar shells, exploding in fury and froth, scattering rocks and shells and detritus up the beach and sucking the sand back into the depths with snakelike hisses.

I'm safe—or at least I think I am. I'm not a palm waiting for the final root-snapping blast. I have the luxury of sheltering in my sandy hollow and watching the spectacle like a young thumb-sucking boy at a circus. And I love it. I almost feel part of the storm's spirit; I'm in the roll and heave of the black waves; I'm in the shrieking wind and the exploding rain-eggs. I'm out of myself and wrapped in the magic and mystery of it all.

✐

What seems like hours later, the calm comes almost as suddenly as the storm. The wind dies. Waves toss in confusion like a restless army without generals and then subside, losing their dour color and adopting, chameleonlike, streaks of their previous blue and turquoise hues.

There are shells and bits of shells everywhere, but they're all empty. Are they merely the discarded garbage of the seabed or have the terrified occupants—conchs, hermit crabs, sea snails—fled to the deeps, abandoning their perfectly formed castles to the fickleness of the surf hordes?

Ridiculous thoughts. The occupants and their castles are complete entities. One can't exist without the other. I've become a hurricane-harassed brain. Can't think straight. But the thought persists. Why are they empty? And so many of them. Wonderful whorls of calcium, so finely etched and colored. Architects and engineers would benefit from studying their microstructure—Corbusian elegances of form-following function; Miesian essays of detail and exactness of fit; Robert Graves's blendings of colors and subtle wit, and a Gaudi-like robustness and flair for sheer arrogance and idiosyncrasy of design. A universe of forms at my feet. A mathematician's total knowledge all in one curled snail shell. Perfect three dimensional geometry. All here.

I thank the storm for its gifts. And then I thank this little island. So compact, so rich, so whole. I am learning something here.

We have to be alone to touch our inner selves. For if we cannot touch ourselves how can we ever truly touch anyone else?

I pick up a shell and stroke it. A thing, so whole, so complete. A product of its own world, its own complex net of dependencies and threats and terrors and truths. And yet, by its very nature—alone. In my hand. And something to take home with me.

John Donne got it right and wrong. "No man is an island" makes sense in a hundred measurable ways. But ultimately we are all islands, and if we don't rejoice in all the possibilities of solitude, we may miss out on one of the primary gifts life gives us.

This island has revived *my* island. This little lost world has given new life to my own personal world. Fears, loneliness, hurricanes, noises in the night...I can accept them all now.

In another day or so, after many more miles of sand and scrub, I'll be meeting Sam again—the boatman who first brought me to the island. I'm looking forward to that. I remember the knowing way in which he caressed and held a frigate bird up in the lagoon where he dropped me off and stretched its wings to show me their size and their beauty. Sam knows and loves this island but he also knows and loves *his* own island, within. There is something complete about the man. A completeness I'm learning to find within myself thanks to a deer, a storm, and a shell.

It is evening again; the sun scatters strands of golden tinsel across the bay. And wisps of silver cloud, pluming—just for me.

A HOMAGE
— To a beach,
a shell
and Frigate bird Sam
— BARBUDA

Thank you, little lost island world.

And here's the letter of thanks I wrote to Frigate Bird Sam:

Dear Sam,

I don't know if you'll ever receive this letter but I felt I had to write to you anyway. Maybe you remember last fall when you took this rather weary Englishman (with a battered backpack and a dream of being alone for a while on a desert island) over to your favorite secret place—the place of the frigate birds and that vast beach, fifteen miles long, with pink talcum sand.

I know we didn't spend much time together. You had a long journey to make back to the mainland in your small boat. But you were patient, you taught me some of the ways of those strange and beautiful birds and you left me on the island in the afternoon and then came back for me five days later down at South Point.

I remember two things in particular. When you left and gave me that great bear-hug you said, "You're going on a bigger journey than you know man, and you'll meet many people!" I was a bit indignant because you'd promised to take me to a place where there were no people at all. And you laughed (I can still hear the sound of your wonderful laugh) and whispered..."there are no people here. Only you...."

And when you came back to pick me up after my utterly amazing five days of solitude, you took one look at my face and you laughed again and said, "Wow man, you looks like you met a real crowd!!"

And boy, were you right. And they were all my crowd. They were all me. And you knew that would happen all along.

Thanks, Sam...for the rest of my life.

Your Friend, David

*All the answers are within us, but such
is our tendency toward forgetting that we
sometimes need to venture to a faraway
land to tap our own memory.*
—HEINRICH ZIMMER

REFLECTIONS

An Ode to Dawdle Days— The Gift of Time

Today, I give myself the gift of time
To wander and wonder and maybe—unwind
Among journeys inwards—the deepest kind
Or to dawdle outwards and drink fine wine
Celebrating the wonders
And that endless gift
of time.

Disappearing Selves —The Power of a Photograph

The best gift is a piece of yourself.

"I have no one to talk to now," said the old man, "except my ghosts."

His ghosts must once have been amazing when this dry, crusted, bone-brittle part of Rajasthan was a Garden of Eden and the tribespeople wore magnificent cloaks of thick, hand-embroidered, mirror-dotted cloth swirled in the brightest of colors and whirled their huge scimitars and double-blade axes in their legendary defense of a beloved homeland.

But almost nothing is left now. The elegantly terraced fields and meticulously laid irrigation channels are mere sandy mounds and collapsed ditches. "There were once great groves of fine trees and cool shade and always the sound of water," the old man had told me when we first met as I drove westward through the pathetic remnants of his once prosperous village. "Palm trees too. Dates. Food—so much food—for all our families."

The land is now virtually devoid of vegetation—a few scrub bushes and cactuslike things, all twisted and seemingly drained of life.

"The camels would come here from far, far away." He swept his wrinkled arm westward toward the vast deserts of Pakistan. "The trading was good. We had beautiful carpets and silks and things made of silver and precious stones. Our women—our mothers, wives, and daughters—all looked so beautiful. We were proud—proud of our families, our villages, our lives. But now..." His voice faded to a dry rasp and he was silent.

Then he lowered his head and I knew he was weeping.

The silence continued for a long time. The heat was like a brazier. There was no shadow, no relief except inside his small mud hut which, for some reason, he avoided during the day, as if something unsettling lay waiting inside.

"The worst thing—and I am sorry, it is not me I weep for but for my people—the worst thing is that I feel that my ghosts are fading, dying, and as I feel them leaving, so I feel I am leaving too."

He looked shriveled, dried up like the land, leached of his memories, drained of the ancestors that were once so much a part of his own spirit.

"I do not think there is much time now," he said in a whisper.

This was one of the hardest departures I've ever made. He'd been so gracious to me during my two days in this desert wasteland, in a village of fallen mud walls and collapsed domed homes. A village of windblown memories—of ghosts now being dissipated by the dying of the land and the dying of this old man.

I wanted to give him something—a gift—something that might bring comfort or hope.

"You told me of your wife," he said as I was preparing to leave. "You seem very happy. You carry her with you inside you as I did with my wife—my family."

"Yes I do," I said. "Anne is very much a part of me and even more so I think when I travel alone."

"May I ask a favor of you?"

"Of course."

"May I see that photograph again—the one of your wife you showed me last evening."

"Absolutely." I pulled out one of the photographs I carry of Anne and which had seemed to strike a chord with him when he first saw it. He now gazed intently again at the small, rather bent and worn image of Anne taken on a journey we had made together during one of our early California backroad odysseys in the seventies. Then he lifted his head and looked straight into my eyes. "Your wife reminds me very much...of my daughter...very beautiful..."

"Really," I said. "I didn't know you had a daughter. I thought..."

"I do not have a daughter now. Not here."

"Here...you mean in this area, in Rajasthan?"

He paused. "No. Not here. On this earth."

"Oh."

"She has gone too. With my wife and all the others. And sometimes now it is difficult to remember..."

"Yes," I said, already knowing what I would do. I had found my gift.

"May I ask you something?" I said.

"Of course. Anything. We have talked of so many things together."

"May I give you this photograph of Anne? It might help you remember your daughter a little better."

He held the little photograph as delicately as a butterfly in his gnarled, wrinkled hands. And then he moved it slowly to rest against his dusty torn robes, above his heart.

I suddenly experienced the oddest sensation. It was as if Anne, the Anne I carry with me always, the Anne who is so much a part of my own spirit, had moved slowly through my body and out and was now resting quietly against this old man's chest, comforting him, passing her love into him, nurturing him in the same way she nurtures me—fully and unconditionally.

As I left he rose, still holding the tiny photograph to his chest, and his eyes were alive and bright. He even seemed to possess her energy now. He held his body proudly, straighter, and looked altogether a bigger man than the increasingly hunched and diminishing person I'd seen for the last two days.

We said nothing more. There really was no need for words or handshakes or hugs or anything else.

Celebrate the music of personal experience of the sacred in those places where it has been known to shine forth. If we are not astounded by these possibilities, we can never plumb the depths of our souls or the soul of the world.
—PHIL COUSINEAU

An Uncle in Us

You carry your family with you, whether you know it or not.

Act 1. Scene 1: Anne and I on our wedding day, a long, long time ago. After our reception we were doing "the rounds" and talking to all our friends and relatives. I spent time with my father's younger brother, Clifford, a man I'd met many times but never really felt I knew. Like many of my family members, he was a rather stoic, self-contained Yorkshireman, unaccustomed to open displays of emotion. But this day was different. He was weeping (in a very Yorkshire way, of course, apart from the rest of the guests and pretending that the sunshine had made his eyes water). He called us both over and asked us to sit down. Then he reached out and held our hands (also rather un-Yorkshire). Tears still filled his eyes and it was obvious that there was something important he needed to say.

"Listen, both of you. I know you don't know me very well

but my whole life has been spent meeting people, day after day. So I can see a few things maybe a bit more clearly than you can. And I can tell you this, without any doubt in my mind at all, that within a year—maybe far less—you'll both be off abroad and you won't be coming home too often, and that you'll both lead lives that most of us—certainly me—can only dream about."

"But, Clifford," I began, "we have no intentions at all of leaving London."

He ignored my interruption, wiped his eyes and said in a soft, almost plaintive voice: "And I want to be a part of your adventures. I've always wanted to travel and see the world. There's an explorer in me, always has been...but, well, things didn't quite work out that way. So, and I know it might seem silly to you two now but someday you'll understand.... I want you to take me with you. I want to know about all your experiences. You don't have to write long letters or make expensive phone calls, just a postcard every once in a while telling me where you are, what you're doing, what the places you're in look and feel like—that's all. Don't make a fuss. Just know that I'm there with you, everywhere you go, and," he laughed, "I won't be any trouble. I promise!"

Later that evening, driving off on our honeymoon saunter around southern England, we remembered Clifford's words and laughed. "I wonder what he meant?" asked Anne. "Who knows?" I replied, and we talked of other things.

✒

Acts 2, 3, 4, and all the rest. Five months later we had packed up our London jobs and were on our way to Tehran. I had been offered—totally unexpectedly—a job with an American company to work on the urban master plan for

Tehran's future growth. We called Clifford to tell him the news and he showed not the least surprise.

"Well, I told you, didn't I?"

"Yes, you did."

"Don't forget—please—make me a little part of your lives, will you, from now on?"

"Yes, Clifford. Yes, we will."

And so we did. Until his death a couple of decades later we would send postcards and spend time with him whenever we made our rather rare trips back home to Yorkshire. And so that's how someone we hardly knew became a small but important part of us and our traveling lives—which continue on, as exciting and intriguing as ever...just as Uncle Clifford had predicted they would.

And Cliff, for the record—you're still with us, in us, and we're still sending you postcards in our heads. Hope you're receiving them.

The moon in the water resembles
the moon in the sky;
The person in the heart is
the person in front of you.
—ANCIENT CHINESE COUPLET

Just Letting Life Happen

If you step out of the way, doors open.

Fleeing a cold Spanish winter, I impulsively loaded my VW camper aboard an enormous ferryboat and plunged southward through Atlantic storms to the Canary Islands, those remote volcanic blips off the west Saharan coast of Africa.

To be sure, my impetuous escape seemed a little bit crazy. I had little in the way of cash—just about enough to return the 700 or so ocean miles to mainland Spain. I knew no one in Gran Canaria, where I alighted, and had no place to stay except for my faithful camper. I didn't know how long I planned to stay or where to go next.

Two days later, the island spoke to me, gently but firmly. "Stay," it said. "Just stay and see what happens." For a person who loves to be on the move, it seemed an odd proposition.

But the voice inside sounded so certain, so totally clear. "Stay. Stay and let things happen."

And so that's what I did. And once I allowed myself to let go, things literally arranged themselves and I stood around watching like a delighted spectator as my life on Gran Canaria was fashioned gently before my eyes.

✐

Although the Canary Islands were referred to briefly by Pliny the Elder as The Fortunate Isles, little was known about these remote volcanic outposts until the arrival of explorer Jean de Béthencourt in 1402, who came with plans to establish colonies for the Spanish Crown. The Guanches, the islands' only inhabitants, were rousted out of their cave-dwelling languor and eliminated long before Columbus's brief but famous stopover here on his way to "discover" the New World.

Gran Canaria and Tenerife experienced the first great surges of tourist-resort development in the 1960s. Little Lanzarote followed later and now boasts a plethora of beach resorts below its moonscape hinterland of volcanoes, lava fields, and "black deserts" of sand and ash.

More remote and undiscovered are the tiny islets of Gomera and Hierro, where dense rainforests and terraced mountains mingle with high sheep pastures, towering volcanoes, and hidden lava-sand beaches. Nobody could tell me much about them or the other outer islands of La Palma and Fuerteventura. I planned to visit them all once I had gained my shore legs after a few days in Las Palmas, the capital of Gran Canaria.

But things didn't quite work out that way.

As I drove out of Las Palmas, the map of the island open but ignored on the passenger seat, I let my camper take the narrow roads at whim. It seemed to know where it was going as we climbed high up the slopes of the largest volcano, Valcequello.

I stopped in a pretty mountain village for tapas in a tiny blue-painted bar with a vine-shaded patio overlooking the whole island. Shall I stay here? I wondered. But I kept on moving.

I drove past more villages with lovely little churches and tiny plazas enclosed by neat white-and-lemon stucco buildings, past banana plantations on terraced hillsides, past vast fields of tomatoes and small vineyards. Huge sprays of bougainvillea burst from roadside hedges. The scent of wild herbs rose from the tiny fields sloping precipitously down to the turquoise ocean.

A tiny cottage appeared with a stone roof in a cleft between two rocks. It had everything: vines, bananas, a small cornfield, two donkeys, blue shutters, and views over cliffs and black volcanic soil beaches and ceaseless lines of surfing ocean.

Here? I wondered. But still I kept moving.

At dusk, I parked on a patch of grass below the volcano. I had some bread, cheese, and sausage, and a glass of brandy, and settled down to sleep feeling utterly at peace. Someone else was orchestrating this trip and that was just fine with me.

Early the next morning, as I sat on a rock watching the sun come up, I looked down and saw something I'd not noticed the night before: a tiny white village huddled on top of a rocky promontory that jutted like an ocean liner straight out into the Atlantic. It was different from anything else I'd seen on the island. Most of the villages were straggly affairs, scattered over hillsides like blown confetti. But this place looked tight and strong and enduring, set on 100-foot cliffs. A long flight of steps climbed up to it from a track. There was no road through the village, just a sinewy path with cubist houses packed

together on either side and ending in an area of level rock at the end of the promontory. I could see laundry blowing in the morning breezes; the hillsides below rose steeply from the rocky beach and were smothered in banana trees. It looked completely cut off from the rest of the island. A true haven.

Somehow the camper groped its way down from the volcano, bouncing and wriggling on cart tracks cut through the brush. I saw no one.

Close up, the village looked even more dramatic. Scores of white-painted steps rose up the rock to the houses that peered down from their cliff-edge niches. Children were playing in the dust at the base of the steps. They stopped and slowly approached, smiling shyly. A rough hand-painted sign nailed to a tree read "El Roque."

"*¡Hola!*" I said.

The children grinned. "*Si, si, hola. ¡Hola!*"

One of the larger boys came over and shook my hand. And he wouldn't let go. He tugged and pointed to the steps. "*Mi casa*—my house. You come."

It was an invitation and I accepted.

We all climbed together. The smaller children straggled in a line behind me; I felt like the Pied Piper and even my wheezing at the end of the 130-step climb had a pipe-ish sound to it.

I've never seen a place quite like El Roque before or since. The lime-white cottages clustered tight in medieval fashion on either side of a six-foot-wide stone path that twisted and roller-coasted up and down, following the idiosyncrasies of the promontory's rocky top. I passed a couple of shops the size of broom closets that doubled as rum bars for the men. Crusty bronzed faces peered out curiously from shadowy doorways. Old women, shrouded in black, scurried by like nervous ravens.

About halfway down the wriggling street we paused outside of the larger houses facing a ten-foot-high carved-wood door decorated with etched brass medallions and a huge door-knocker in the shape of a lion's head. The older boy, obviously one of the leaders of my pack of frisky followers, pushed at the door and a panel squeaked open. The rest of the door remained solidly in place.

We entered a dark lobby with bare blue walls and a richly tiled floor. The boy took my hand and gestured to his followers to stay back at the main door. We moved deeper into the house where it was even darker. Then he opened a smaller door and the sunshine rushed in, blinding me.

We were in the living room, classically decorated with small tapestries, a broad oak table on bulbous legs, topped with two fat brass candlesticks encased in wax drippings. Eight dining chairs were placed around the table, their backs and sides carved in high baroque style with vine leaves and grape bunches. Straight ahead were three large windows looking out over a bay of black sand edged by banana plantations and, beyond that, the great cone of Valcequello. The room was filled with light. The windows were open and I could hear birds—canaries, I thought, by their flighty chattering, and mourning doves issuing soft cooing sounds.

The boy's name was Julio. He called out and I could hear someone coming, the swish of sandals on tiles. I was still mesmerized by the view until a figure stepped in front of me and gave a slight curtsy. She was utterly—devastatingly—beautiful. "My sister," said Julio in slow English. "She is named Maria."

Another door opened and the room suddenly became much smaller. A great bear of a man entered, hands as big as frying pans and fingers like thick bananas. A bushy mustache covered most of his mouth and curved down, walruslike, at either side. His hair was as black and bushy as his mustache. A long scar reaching from forehead to jawbone gave him a dangerous look but his eyes were the gentlest blue, shining, exuding welcome without words.

Julio stood, rake-straight, Maria gave one of her curtsies and vanished and I came around the table to meet the man. "Papa, this is Señor David."

Tomas Feraldes could speak no English but during the next

half hour or so I had one of the richest conversations I've ever had with a stranger. His words rumbled from deep in his chest, like boulders tumbling down a ridge. His son acted as interpreter and we talked in baby-language of everything—the village, his banana plantation upon which all the villagers depended for their livelihoods, the ocean, the wonderful variety of fish you could catch from the promontory cliffs, the history of Gran Canaria, and the great pride of the islanders in their little green paradise.

"We are of Spain but we are not of Spain," he told me. "We are Canary people. This is our land. This is our country."

The brandy flowed. Little dishes appeared—*calamares* in lemon and garlic, big fat fava beans that we squeezed to pop out the soft flesh, spicy mixes of tomatoes and garlic with chunks of lime-marinated fish, sardines, island cheeses and, of course, more brandy.

Then Julio turned to me. "My father says you will stay here if you wish."

"Here? Where? In this house?"

"No—in another place. My brother's home. He is away in Madrid."

"Where is this house?"

"It is very close. My father says you will come to see your house now. If you wish."

I now knew I had no control over anything. I'd followed my inner voice and let things happen and they were happening so fast and so perfectly I had no wish to impede the flow.

We were outside again in the narrow street. The children were still there, and off we all went, Pied-Piper fashion again, wriggling between the houses. We walked right to the end of the promontory where we all stood on the edge of the towering cliffs, watching huge waves explode fifty feet in the air and feeling their vibrations through the rock.

Julio nudged me. "This is your house." He was pointing to a small square building, the last house on the rock, white and blue, with a staircase leading up to a red door. On the flat roof I could see plants waving. There were windows everywhere overlooking the beach, the volcano, the broad Atlantic.

Grinning like an idiot again, I followed him up the stairs. He unlocked the door and we walked into one of the most beautiful rooms I have ever seen. Light filled every niche. On the left was a small propane stove, a sink, a big working table, and four van Gogh-styled chairs with straw seats.

The living area was simply furnished—a few scattered rugs, armchairs, low tables, lamps and empty shelves, hungry for books. I could see the bathroom tiled in blue Spanish tiles and then another staircase leading up and out onto the roof with views over everything—the whole village, ocean, mountains, bays. It was a dream.

"You like your home?" Julio was watching my face.

"Julio, this the best house I have ever seen."

Moving in was splendid chaos. Every child in the village came to help me carry my belongings from the camper (it looked so tiny from the top of those 130 steps) to the house at the end of the village—clothes, sleeping bag, cameras, food, fishing rod, cushions, towels—and my guitar. When the children saw it, they went wild. Compared to the tiny ukulele-like island *timpales,* this was a brute of an instrument, a battered Gibson with a rich deep tone. They were all shouting something at me. Indispensable Julio stepped in again.

"They say play, Señor David. Please."

Oh, what the heck. So I began... "Skip, skip, skip to m'Lou..."

I'd used the same song before on my journeys, and it had worked wonders. The chorus is simple, the melody obvious, and even if you can't get the words straight, you can hum and la-la all the way through it. Which is precisely what they all did.

Twenty-three little voices sang lustily at the bottom of El Roque's steps, in the hot afternoon sun. High above, a crowd of villagers who had gathered by the wall at the top of the rock began clapping, and then the kids started clapping. Soon the whole bay rang to the sound of this crazy ditty that was utterly meaningless to them and perfect for an impromptu getting-to-know-you celebration on this, my first day in my new home at El Roque.

It was months before I left Gran Canaria. I even managed to tempt Anne to put aside her work for a while and join me in my island home.

The villagers were delighted. Once they realized I was married, all attempts were abandoned to match me up with one of the many eligible females in El Roque (no, Julio's sister, Maria, was already spoken for). And on the day Anne arrived, I invited the whole village to the house for a celebration. I had no idea what a Pandora's box I'd opened with this innocent little gesture.

I'd asked everyone to come over in the evening after their long workday on the banana plantation. Any time after six, I said. Anne and I prepared some platters of bread and cheese and opened bottles of island wine and rum. Then at 6:30 precisely, there was a knock on the door. It was Julio (he'd long since appointed himself as my social secretary and general factotum).

"Please come. We are all welcoming your Mrs. David."

Anne and I walked out on the platform at the top of our steps and looked down. Faces! Scores of laughing, smiling Canary faces staring up at us, clapping, singing. And everyone was carrying something—we could see cakes, pans of broiled fish, a flailing sack of crabs (still very much alive), banana branches, straw baskets of tomatoes, bottles of wine, and more cakes.

"Everyone who comes to the house must bring present," Julio told us. "It is our custom."

I have no idea how we got the whole village of El Roque into our tiny house, but we did. The kitchen, the living room, even the roof was jammed with villagers—many of them we'd never met. Anne and I were buoyed like froth ahead of the surge onto the roof, and we never made it back to the kitchen to serve the simple dishes we'd prepared. Someone carried up the *timpales* and the guitar and off we went into a spree of folk songs that set the whole house bouncing long into the night.

What had been intended as a one-time "Welcome to Mrs. David" occasion became a regular weekly event for the rest of our stay. Every Thursday evening there'd be a "folk-fest" gathering at the house that would leave our voices hoarse and our kitchen table bowed with food. The problem was not in feeding the multitudes but in actually getting rid of all the fish, sausages, tomatoes, bananas, crabs, cakes, and wine before the next session on the following Thursday.

The most difficult items were the bananas. They'd bring whole branches with as many as 150 firm green bananas hanging from them. We tried every way we could think of to use them—banana bread, banana cake, banana crêpes, banana omelet, banana purée, banana soufflé, fried bananas, banana with garlic, and cream-mashed (like potatoes, interesting experiment there), even fish with baked whole bananas. And we still ended up with huge surpluses.

Aside from the rent we insisted on giving Julio's father each month (which he promptly and laughingly refunded in bottles of local rum), we were living a cash-free life. We were utterly happy in our village and had no real desire to go anywhere else on the island. I found great satisfaction in painting again, something I'd let slide, and Anne discovered a previously unknown gift for knitting enormous, six-foot-long woolen shawls in rainbow colors.

Every couple of weeks we'd pack a box of these creations, leap into the camper, and drive the thirty or so bumpy miles into Las Palmas to sell our work to bored tourists with lots of money and very little to spend it on. Not that we needed the money—but it was rewarding to see people willing to pay real cash for our rooftop creations.

Our village had dignity, pride and constant pep. If there were family problems, we never saw them. If there was malicious gossip and backbiting, it must have been taking place well off the main path that we walked every day. If there was infidelity and illicit romance, it was done with such craft and guile as to be unnoticeable.

El Roque was a true home, and we became as close to the villagers as our natures could allow. We went fishing and crab-hunting with the men (the latter at night with huge torches of reeds dipped in tar that drew the crabs from the rocks like magnets—all we had to do was pick them up and pop them into hessian sacks). We picked mini-mountains of tomatoes, we painted portraits of the villagers and gave them as gifts, we learned how to prepare the rich sauces for Canary Island fish dishes, and we even learned to love bananas in all their culinary variations.

But most important of all, the village brought us a peace and revealed far more creative selves than we'd ever experienced before and have only rarely enjoyed since. Anne suddenly found herself writing fragments of poetry, songs—even singing occasionally—making bread, experimenting with the guitar, and teaching English to some of the older children.

I too was amazed at what emerged from within. I did more sketching than I'd ever done before and experimented with a whole mélange of styles and techniques. And then came the cartoonist, the autobiographer, the photographer, the creative "improv" cook, the furniture maker, and even a period of origami!

Our newly emerging selves rejoiced in their relief and we watched in wonder as we just...let life happen.

El Roque is, and will always remain, a touchstone of revelations for us both.

Don't play for safety—it's the most dangerous game in the world.
—HUGH WALPOLE

PUB PEARLS

The Noosphere

*The British pub, that most egalitarian of social institutions, mimicked but never quite matched anywhere else in the world, is the ideal place for gleaning fragments of overheard insights and little wisdoms (not necessarily recognized as such by the speakers!). On a recent journey through England I began, for no particular reason except that I find pubs fascinating, to produce a series of sketches evoking their unique charms. And during pauses inside each of them for necessary liquid refreshments I'd intentionally listen for any tidbits of interesting conversations and scribble down the dialogue as best I could. Many of these notes, when reread the morning after, failed to live up to my hopes of illuminating perceptions. But a few did, and I share these throughout the book as little revelations—**Pub Pearls**—of our sometimes amusing, sometimes sad, but always fascinating human condition.*

"Y'see the basic dilemma is whether there is a moral super-structure—a genetically implanted master plan—that makes us recognize the inevitability of our teleological instinct...."

"Teleological?"

"....Our inbred instinct to merge—to evolve if you will, as presumably all other species have done—into a composite whole, the inevitable manifest destiny of a common goal—a state that Teilhard de Chardin referred to as the Noosphere."

"Noosphere?"

"The ultimate purpose of the human species, us, the highest species evolution to date according to Darwin and others, is to break through all our petty barriers and synthetic provocations and distractions—wars, conflicts, revolutions, class-structures and all that—and to recognize and fulfill our ultimate collective human potential of the unified mind, the unified soul."

"And shopping too?"

"What??"

"Shopping. That's one of our many distractions."

"Oh...right. Shopping could definitely be considered a reflection of our tendency toward aimless distractions."

"And TV."

"Oh yes. Definitely TV. And talking of TV, did you see that show the other night with old Tom Jones?"

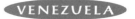

Almost Gone #2
Tepuy-Terrors

*Carelessness can be a teacher, too, so learn from
your own mistakes.*

I was deep in among Venezuela's Gran Sabana *tepuis*—those
amazing vertical-sided monoliths, thousands of feet high, that
rise out of the incredibly dense rainforest in the nation's southern sector. Two Pémon Indian guides, Tin and Pan (yes—those
were their names—or at least the ones they gave me when we
first met), had taken me in their *curiare* canoe along winding
and ever-narrowing streams overhung by the dark, hot jungle,
into the eastern fringes of *tepuy* country way beyond Angel
Falls. I'd explained to them that I'd like to climb one of the
smaller *tepuis* (not with pitons and ropes, I said; it had to be
something I could "scramble" up) and explore its summit
which, like all the *tepuis*, would be basically a plateau, cut into

fissures and mini-canyons by the almost constant rain that falls from an almost equally constant cloud cover.

They knew of one *tepuy*, they told me, that they thought could be climbed, although they had not done so themselves. When I asked them why, they explained reluctantly that "bad spirits" may be up there, and things...creatures...which may be very dangerous. And I smiled. This was precisely the notion that Sir Arthur Conan Doyle had used in his non-Sherlock Holmes novel, *The Lost World*, when he surmised correctly that these virtually untouched "islands in the sky" would be Darwinian paradises—aerial Galápagoses—where species of plants and animals could evolve relatively undisturbed by other environments into completely new forms or at least variations of known life. Of course, to give his popular novel added drama, he assumed such forms to be enormous, prehistoric dinosaurlike species, which then, of course, helped inspire the film of the same name.

I however did not expect to see such exotica and would, I told myself, be perfectly content with an unusual butterfly or two.

And so we left. It was a long two days of travel and as we approached our isolated *tepuy*, the view became more elusive. Occasionally it would rear up like a vast totem over the trees. But most times it was hidden behind jungle curtains or in thick cloud cover with only its dark base exposed.

After storing the canoes well away from the turbulent river and climbing the lower flanks of the *tepuy*, we lost sight of it altogether. The jungle closed in around us. Tin and Pan improvised a trail through the scratching palm scrub and dangling vines. We were ascending, so at least we were headed in the right direction. But the *tepuy* gave us no clues. Having beckoned us from afar it now ignored us as we flailed around its lower muddy slopes.

Then finally we had our first real moment of contact. Tin was leading us up along a streamed full of tiny waterfalls and still, black pools. It was a wet, tiring slog with no rhythm to it all—slime-coated rocks, unreliable handholds, and a couple of dousings. I was getting rather fed up with the whole idea of this journey until the jungle suddenly drew back, light tumbled into a clearing, and filigrees of waterfalls, like floating gossamer, rained down on us.

We looked up and there she was, all 2,000 feet of her, rising straight up into a clear sky. She looked magnificent—but there seemed to be no obvious way up. The walls were too sheer. It was a beautiful and very depressing sight. My legs decided they'd had enough and buckled. I felt like a reluctant and doltish plodder and just wanted to sleep. So we set up camp and that was about all I remember of that day.

Early the following morning the rock face had vanished again, and the dainty waterfalls floated down out of thick clouds. Maybe it was better that we couldn't see the impossibility of the climb, otherwise I might have given up and stayed in camp. But I felt optimistic, so off we went.

Sometimes at night I wake in a cold sweat, remembering that experience. First of all I am not a mountaineer. Ropes and pitons and fancy, claw-soled boots hold no appeal whatsoever. I'm a scrambler. Give me boulders and bits of root to cling to and I'll improvise a way to the top eventually. And, to be honest, most of the climb was precisely that. Edging and squeezing our way up deep clefts in the *tepuy* and cursing the black mossy slime that seemed to coat everything—rocks, trees, bushes, and most of our bodies.

But there was one occasion when I thought my nerve would snap and I'd have to admit ignominious defeat. It happened—as most disasters do—without warning. I was getting a little cocky, not to say foolhardy, as my scrambling techniques seemed to be working and the summit edged closer. I should have seen the warning signs—loose rocks and leaky moss doused in rivulets of running water. Tin and Pan were ahead and had negotiated that little section of the *tepuy* apparently without qualms. Maybe they'd unwittingly loosened the rocks or the moss. All I remember was that one moment I was rejoicing in the sweet smell of upcoming success, and the next second the ground gave way beneath both feet and I felt myself start an

impromptu descent with my flailing arms reaching out for something to grab. You've never experienced the essence of helplessness until you begin sliding slowly—horribly slowly—downhill on a slime-coated rock, with no handholds around and no way of stopping yourself, towards the edge of a 1,000-foot drop into total oblivion.

It was the slowness of it all that still sends tingles to my toes, and the absolute predictability of my fate. I'm not exactly sure even now how I escaped except that by rolling slightly to my left I found a pocket of rock uncoated by the slime and used that as a brake. By the time my slide had stopped I could feel the updraft of air on the vertical side of the *tepuy* rushing past my face.

I decided not to dwell on the possibilities. If my confidence went, then the whole little expedition would have been a wasted effort. So I concentrated on the climb; one more cleft, a narrow ledge swirled in the mist, then an easier stretch up a forty-five-degree incline, then a cleft again. On and on and on. I never knew that 2,000 feet could seem so far.

But the summit was all I'd hoped for and more—a barren black wilderness of worn rocks, as remote and bleak a landscape as you can imagine. Another world, another planet.

And as if to welcome us, the clouds vanished and we floated in limbo. Above, nothing but blue in all directions; below, a cotton-ball landscape of low clouds cutting out views of the jungle. And rising like fantasy castles in the distance, the other great *tepuis* themselves, enormous islands in the sky, all flat topped, each one unique in bulk and profile, ancient keeps of ancient life forms, untouched and unexplored since the beginning of time. I thanked Sir Arthur Conan Doyle again for tempting me here, to the solitude and majesty of this amazing lost world.

According to my map, the summit of our *tepuy* was roughly circular and only a mile or so across from one rim to the other, a relatively modest island compared to many of the others we could see. I'd hoped to spend a couple of days up here but hadn't realized how cold it would be. In spite of the open skies and brilliant midday sun, it was hard to keep warm in the biting wind that screeched across the black rocks.

Tin and Pan showed little interest in exploring. They found a small hollow behind one of the eroded pillars and, using their hammocks as blankets, huddled together, looking frozen and forlorn.

I was too excited to sit and told them I'd be back shortly after a little alfresco exploring among the shadowy clefts. They nodded glumly and huddled closer together.

Based on cursory studies of this virtually unexplored region, botanists estimate there may be as many as four thousand plant forms unique to these summits. No dinosaurs, no pterodactyls, no wild tribes of missing-link ape men such as Conan Doyle fantasized, but at least he was right in principle. The isolation of the *tepuis* has given us a living laboratory of hitherto unknown species.

At first I saw few signs of life anywhere. The clefts between the eroded pillars were damp, puddled, and bare. At one point I had to squeeze sideways to pass between the monoliths only to find myself peering straight down a deep fissure that seemed to have no bottom. A small stream trickled off a ledge and disappeared, doubtless reappearing as a lacy waterfall out the side of the *tepuy* hundreds of feet below. Here I found rich little groupings of lichen and mini-succulents and a cluster of brilliant red flowers, only an inch or so across, with yellow-edged petals. Flycatchers.

Moving deeper into the labyrinth I lost track of time. Carelessly I'd left my watch back in my rucksack with the guides and was so enamored with the possibility of being the first explorer of this unknown world that I'd failed to notice the change in the weather. It had become much darker. The blue sky had been replaced by clouds, not the happy puffball variety, but that cloying gray mist again, wrapping its chilly tentacles around the tops of the black pillars and sinewing through the clefts.

I'd mentally registered a series of distant rocky landmarks into the labyrinth, but now it all seemed very different. I decided to go back to the starting point on the rim of the *tepuy* and see how bad the cloud cover really was. The idea of having my explorations cut short by a bit of mist was ridiculous.

I found the flycatchers without any problem but couldn't see far enough ahead to the next reference point. Somewhere in the gloom was a protrusion shaped like an ape's head. At least that's what it looked like from the other side, but not from here.

One cleft on my right seemed familiar so I edged my way between the rock walls for a hundred feet or so until it ended abruptly. There were enough handholds to scale the wall. Maybe I'd be able to see my starting point from the top.

Covered in moss and mud I eased myself up into a world of whirling mist and nothing else. I retreated into the cleft and back to the reassuring clump of flycatchers. Only they weren't *my* flycatchers. There were only three of them and they were the wrong color.

O.K. Hold on. No reason to panic. Just a slight error of orientation. If only I could find the ape's head. I can't be more than a hundred yards from the rim.

Then came the thunder. It began as a gentle stomach rumble way off among the *tepuis*, then headed straight for the labyrinth with ground-cracking fury and climaxed in a shattering roar right over my head.

Enough! Time to panic.

I matched the thunder blow for blow. Between the booms I roared out the names of my guides into the mist. (Tin and Pan. How ridiculous can you get?) Nothing. Another boom. More name calling. Boom! Tin! Boom! Pan! More nothing.

I was angry with my bubble-brained antics and my waddlesome sloth, with my guides, with the thunder, with this stupid maze of rocks. I was so angry I almost stepped into the fissure with the little disappearing stream.

What a wonderful fissure! What a lovely little stream! Now at least I knew where I was.

And the guides were just where I'd left them, fast asleep, oblivious of all the din and the cold mist swirling about them.

"Tin, where's my bag?"

I was a bit rough in waking him but was peeved he'd been peacefully dozing while I was losing my marbles in the labyrinth. He'd been using my bag as a cushion and handed it to me sheepishly. I decided not to tell him about my lousy sense of direction and fumbled instead for my watch. It was 2 P.M. We had five, maybe six hours of light left. I wanted to stay on the summit but felt decidedly unwelcome now.

"Can we get back down to the trees in five hours?"

Two sleepy heads nodded enthusiastically. Their hammocks were rolled in seconds, stuffed into their bags, and they were ready. Eager. If it had been a cultural norm, I think they might even have kissed me.

One last look. The mist was still swirling around the black rocks. So much to learn up here. So much to discover. These islands in the sky don't relinquish their secrets easily. The careless will be punished, and I'd been too careless by half already. I prayed for a safe descent and an uneventful return to the comforts of our camp.

A soft bed, a decent meal and a few cold beers suddenly seemed very appealing. I'd already pushed my everyday self into new nooks and crannies both for the body and mind, and for the moment, that was more than enough.

Unless you leave room for serendipity, how can the divine enter in? The beginning of the adventure of finding yourself is to lose your way.
—JOSEPH CAMPBELL

The Synergism of Little Kindnesses

Be generous—it's the natural thing to do,
and it comes back in equal measure.

༄

It was approaching Christmastide in Italy's Abruzzi Mountains, which could explain this series of small but oh-so-significant events. Or maybe not. Actually I believe they could happen anytime...all it takes is that first little spontaneous act of kindness to set the whole synergistic, cause-and-effect magic into almost endless, rippling motion.

༄

I was stuck. My camper had broken down in a forest in these wild Apennine ranges that swirl and buckle their tortuous way down the length of the country, virtually to its very toe at Reggio di Calabria. After a bit of pathetic fiddling and banging and cursing (I'm not much of a mechanic. That particular self must be unusually deep or has been purposely hiding away for decades), I decided I was likely to be here until morning. I'd seen very little in the way of traffic, discounting something resembling a wolf that, at dusk, slipped boldly out of the forest and stood watching me for an unnerving length of time, and two well-lubricated youths on those ghastly moped things that firecracker around every nook and cranny of this otherwise delightful country.

But I was wrong. Someone was coming in a car. The driver stopped at my insistent waving and got out, all smiles and seasonally happy, took one look at my "foreign" engine, and said he'd take me to the next village, about ten miles down the road.

He dropped me off at the only gas station in the place and refused any offer on my part of a thank-you gift—money, a cigar, a bar of chocolate, which were all I had with me. He explained my predicament to the mechanic, a middle-aged woman. In no time the woman and I were beetling back up into the forest in her tow truck. She seemed amused by me or by my appearance or something. And then I understood. "You—San' Claus," she giggled. "Big!" She rubbed her stomach. "Ver' white!" She pointed to my beard. I nodded and smiled. This had happened before on my journeys but not until, for some odd reason, my once Irish-auburn beard had suddenly turned completely white a couple of years back despite the fact that my head hair remained exactly as ever—a kind of bog-country brown.

We arrived at the camper. Nimble as a chipmunk she was out with her bag of tricks and literally, within three minutes, had the creature purring contentedly again with none of the banging and cursing and expletives-deleted that had accompanied my useless efforts.

Again I offered payment. She refused and giggled once more at my appearance. "Just like San' Claus!" before scrambling back into her truck and suggesting I follow her back into the village.

Well, that was one problem solved. Next was food—a bakery for some bread for dinner. And cakes. Gorgeous cream and chocolate delights just begging to be eaten on the spot. I congratulated the baker on his fantastic array of chocablock-calorie cannoli and he was apparently so pleased at my compliments and my efforts at Italian 101 vernacular that he presented me with an extra little hazelnut and caramel vanilla-cream puff-pastry creation in its own little box. His wife stood by nodding and grinning. I thanked him profusely and moved on to the next store, a pharmacy, to buy some supplies for a cold I felt coming on. Again, as soon as I walked in, the Santa Claus routine started up and the two older women behind the counter put on little girl faces and asked, "Where are our presents?!" So I played along, wondering what I could give them that might have a little of the seasonal spirit in it. And of course—what better than the boxed masterpiece of confectionery presented to me by the baker and his wife?

"Have you been very, very good?" I asked in my deepest Santa voice. "Oh yes, yes! Ver', ver' good," they responded in delighted Italglish as I gave them the cake and left the store buoyed on waves of giggles and gasps of delight. Suddenly a hand was at my elbow. One of the women was tugging me back inside and the other one, coyly and shyly, came around the counter with something behind her back. "For you," she said and handed me a large box of chocolates all adorned in Christmas motifs. I tried to refuse but they'd have none of it. "No, no—you take—eat..." and they nudged me back into the street, still giggling, "San' Claus need," and they patted their stomachs like kids.

A box of Italian chocolates! What a lovely surprise. I opened them up and twenty beautifully decorated bonbons stared expectantly up at me. What a splendid addition to my dinner. Except...no, they weren't really mine. I had people to thank. So back I went to the bakery and showed them the chocolates and asked them to help themselves. They were delighted and carefully chose one each. "No, no!" I said. "Please take more." And after much encouragement I persuaded them to take six—and then there was one more for an old man coming into the store for his evening loaf. He almost lost his balance, he was so surprised.

And then the mechanic lady. I went to the end of main street and there she was, busy with someone else's car. "Aha!" she grinned. "San' Claus!"

"Yes," I said. "And here's a little gift specially for you," and I made her take half a dozen chocolates.

So that left seven chocolates. Still too many for me. I asked if she knew the man who had given me the lift into town in the first place. She nodded but was not sure where he lived.

So I went out onto the street again, chocolate box rampant and in real Santa Claus mode (I was beginning to enjoy this role now). I handed out one chocolate each to any stranger who had the semblance of a smile. Which was just about everyone I met, so my seven chocolates rapidly diminished to one. "Mine!" I thought, and salivated.

And then, who should I see coming down the village main street with his dog but the man who first helped me back in the forest. I pushed the box at him, tried to apologize for only having a single chocolate to offer, and almost bludgeoned him into accepting it.

And that, I thought, was that.

But no. I was wrong. The man, who fortunately could speak a little more English than most of the villagers, invited me to accompany him for a drink at his local trattoria which, of course, I willingly accepted, and this, believe it or not, led me to one of the best weeks I've ever had in Italy. For, it turned out, this man was the bocci champion of the village (apparently a

position of considerable prestige) and he decided San' Claus needed a place to rest to enjoy the abundance of the season. Which I did and which is a whole other tale. Suffice to say, for a few days, the village took me in and made me part of itself, sharing its festive joy, its food and drink, and its heart—many, many hearts—and all because of that man's one tiny act of spontaneous kindness way back in the forest.

I am circling and circling...
Am I a falcon, a storm, or a great song?
—RAINER MARIA RILKE

A Whack of Wordsworth

On a recent meander through the Lake District of Britain, I came across Dove Cottage, an ancient, bent, beamed and bowed ex-tavern where the poet William Wordsworth had lived with his sister Dorothy, and hosted a panoply of renowned poets, authors, artists, and men of letters.

William Wordsworth is England's "mother's milk" poet—everyone's been nurtured on "The Daffodils" and his other beloved pastoral poems. But he had a deeper, darker side that saw life as a grinding-down process slowly and inevitably eradicating the knowledge, purity, and sense of universal immortality with which we were born—that intuitive understanding of the endless recycling of life and energy of which we are all eternally a part.

Deep down, we know so much more than we dare admit— we knew that we are far more complex and amazing than we dare dream. Except of course in the rich dreams of infancy.

I'd avoided Wordsworth's poetry since indoctrination and overkill at high school—but wandering through the small, simple rooms and reading handwritten manuscripts littered with his scrawly editings and inkblots from his bro-

HAWKSHEAD 8/00 — ENGLAND'S LAKE DISTRICT
HERE WORDSWORTH ATTENDED SCHOOL . . .

ken quill pen, I rediscovered the richness, depth and the soulful insightfulness of his thoughts and words. The following
lines leapt off their yellowed parchment pages....
From "Ode: Intimations of Immortality"

Our Birth is but a sleep and a forgetting;
the soul that rises with us, our life's star,
hath had elsewhere its setting
and cometh from afar;
Not in entire forgetfulness
and not in utter nakedness
but trailing clouds of glory do we come
from God, who is our home.
Heaven lies about us in our infancy!

The Kumbh Mela— A Bath for Fifteen Million People

You can find your own holy man within you if you open up to the secrets of others.

The ultimate cleansing of body and spirit! At Allahabad in north central India one splash, paddle, and body-wash in the fast-flowing Ganges—the holy mother of rivers—at the right moment of the right day "reaps the benefit of bathing on ten million solar eclipse days." It's an offer any self-respecting Hindu cannot possibly refuse. A whole lifetime of sin, debauch, and spiritual uncenteredness washed away in a few wet moments. A new beginning, a promise of eternal bliss, salvation, Nirvana!

"You should see the Kumbh Mela at Allahabad," I'd been advised by a friend in Kathmandu. "It's an incredible festival of cleansing. Fifteen million people—all coming to the Ganges once every twelve years. Incredible. You might just make it. It's worth a try!"

So I tried. And I made it.

From a distance it looks like a vast military encampment: thousands of square white tents with four-sided pyramidal roofs lined up in endless rows filling the dusty flats around the Triveni Sangam, the confluence of the three rivers. (You can actually see only two but in India nothing is what it seems and everyone insists that it is the third, invisible river of Saraswati that endows this place with unique significance.)

It's very hot. A white dust hangs in a cloud over the site, giving a haloed, mystic feeling. I've been walking for almost an hour now from the cordoned-off entrance to the Sangam. Actually, *walking* is not quite the word, more like half-carried, half-trampled by a thick mélange of humanity filling the hundred-foot-wide "corridors" between the tents and the fenced encampments of the sadhus, the gurus, the *sanyasins,* and the swamis. Each encampment has its own ceremonial entrance made up of rickety scaffolding and tied bamboo poles topped with painted symbols, logos, and depictions of Hindu deities. A vast supermarket of salvation specialists. Hundreds of them from all over India, each surrounded by his own faithful disciples and followers. The women in their bright saris feverishly cook and clean outside the square tents, while the men, bearded, ascetic, and clad in *dhotis* or dark robes, gather in hunched groups around their chosen wise man to listen and debate and nod and sleep and listen again.

And the crowd churns on. Once in it's almost impossible to break free without the risk of being squashed to a sweaty pulp by a million shoeless and sandaled feet. I'm not even sure where we're going but I'm part of the flow, and there's nothing I can do to stop it.

"Are you understanding the significance, sir, of this event, sir?"

A young man in long white robes links his arm in mine and smiles brightly into my dust-smeared face.

I don't really feel like talking (I'm far too busy trying not to trip on the pebbly track), and I mumble something about having read an article in *The Times of India.*

The youth smiles sympathetically. "Ah, *The Times*, sir. That is a good paper. But I think it is possible that you don't understand everything, sir. It is a very long history."

"Yes," I mumble again. "Yes, I suppose it is." Everything in India has a long history.

"My name is Raj, sir, and I will tell you much about the history of Kumbh Mela if you wish."

So he did (far too much to include here) but after what seemed like an eternity of recitations about gods and kings and myths and legends, he could see I was losing interest and his face took on a mischievous look.

"Would you like something secret to see, sir?"

I looked up. Among the crowds were the occasional Western faces, the faces of seekers, coming to the *mela* to find answers to all the mysteries, coming to find comfort, coming to "play with God," coming to experience the "perfectly conscious religious life."

Singing, chanting, dancing, and discordant sitar sounds exploded from a score of pavilions. Babies rolled in the sand while sari-clad mothers washed and polished huge copper rice cauldrons at the water taps; ancient hermitlike men displayed themselves in the most contorted positions in little tents with hand-painted signs nailed to bamboo posts: *Guru Ashanti has sat in this same position without moving for eight years. Rastan Jastafari eats only wild seeds and drinks one glass of goat's milk every eight days to the honor of Shiva.* A fairground of fakirs! There were men with necklaces of cobras and pythons; a troupe of dancing monkeys playing brass cymbals; scores more fortune-tellers with their little trained birds; and countless peanut vendors.

There were special compounds for Tamils, for Tibetan refugees, for Nepalese pilgrims from the high Dolpo region of the Himalayas, for ascetic members of the Jain religion and for a hundred other far more obscure sects.

After all this hullabaloo and crush, my little guide's idea appealed.

"Fine, Raj. Great idea!" Anything to escape the increasingly claustrophobic throngs.

"So—please come!"

He led me deeper and deeper into the mazelike mass of tents and impromptu shelters and enormous canvas structures for devotees until I had lost all my bearings.

"Almost at the place, sir," Raj whispered encouragingly and put a finger over his lips. "Please—we must be quiet."

Deeper and deeper in we went. The tents were separated by dusty little snaking alleyways, barely wide enough for a single person. And then a wall of sorts, thrown together with adobe and lath, and with a sign painted in large crude Xs, presumably meaning "go away—get lost!" Raj peered through a minuscule crack in the wall and whispered, "Please—you look now." So I peeped too. And sitting in a comfortable huddle of cloaks and turbans and robes were half a dozen or so distinguished gurulike gentlemen, some with enormous beards, sharing a meal and laughing together like longtime buddies having a little time off together. I shrugged my shoulders questioningly to Raj. "They are all very famous men—wise men—from all different parts of India," he whispered.

"A gathering of gurus!" I said, trying to add a little levity to our Peeping Tom antics.

"Please," he warned. "We should not be here. The men—each has thousands, maybe millions of followers. All different sects of peoples."

"So, they're really competitive? In the religious business."

Raj smiled.

"Well, they don't look like they're competing much," I said.

Raj giggled softly. "Not competitors—all together. All the same. People think they different. They say—my guru better than your guru—but gurus know—they all the same, all together, friends."

I imagined a Monty Python take on their laconic conversings:

"We're trying a novel idea this year, Fred—instant enlightenment in a month. A thousand lifetimes is too long for most people. Special deal for Americans—two weeks! They have short vacations!"

A gaggle of shared giggles.

"And Jack—how's the new ashram going?"

"Harry, if you're not using that cave of yours up on Annapurna for a year or two, I wonder—"

"Got any more of that holy water Dick?"

I felt a little guilty thinking such disrespectful, un-Kumbh-Mela thoughts, but Raj and I both snuck away chuckling.

⌐

Later, in a more serious, reflective mood (the intensity and obvious importance of this event to millions of people had begun to sink in), I sat on a bluff overlooking the merger of the two rivers. The sun sank, an enormous orange globe squashing into the horizon, purpling the dust haze, gilding the bodies of the bathers.

The moon rose, big, fat, and silver in a cobalt evening sky. There were thousands of people by the river now. The bathing increased but everything seemed to be in slow motion. I watched one old man, almost naked, progress through the careful rituals of washing. He was hardly visible through the throng, and yet he acted as if he were the only person there by the river, unaware of everything but the slow steady rhythms of his cleansing. After washing every part of his body he began to clean his small brass pitcher, slowly rubbing it with sand, polishing the battered metal with a flattened twig, buffing its rough surface with a wet cloth, until it gleamed in the moonlight. He looked very old, very emaciated, and held that pitcher as if it were his only possession, which, quite possibly, it was. Then he disappeared and other bodies took his place by the river.

I sensed timelessness and began to feel the power of this strange gathering. Each person performed the rituals in his or her own way, and yet from a distance there seemed to be a mystical unity among all of them, all these souls as one soul, cleansing, reviving, touching eternity in the flow of the wide black river, linking with the infinity, becoming part of the whole of which we are all a part.

I made my way slowly to the river and knelt down. For a moment there was no me left in me. The river, the people, the movements, the night breeze, the moon, life, death, all became as one continuum. A smooth, seamless totality. An experience beyond experience. A knowingness beyond knowledge.

I washed my face and arms and let the water fall back to the flowing river, where it was carried away into the night.

> *The greatest gift you can give the world*
> *is your own growth into the full consciousness*
> *of your own possibilities—and ultimately*
> *the evolutionary possibilities of the*
> *whole human species.*
> —ALAN WATTS

Into the Light

All this talk of "enlightenment"
of gurus, shaktis, and deep insightfulment
gives me headaches and even frightenment
when (it seems to me)
it's all just our natural entitlement
to step into the light, just as the Creator meant
us to do
the light that's already burning bright
in me
and
in
you.

We Shall Live Again

Ancient wisdom resides around each bend in the road.

Deep in the mountains of Oregon, way back in the Klamath Ranges, I'd journeyed on back roads so faint and occasionally nonexistent that I wondered if I'd ever find my way out again. I wasn't exactly lost. Or maybe I was. Maybe I wanted to be lost, to be utterly vulnerable, to be open to whatever came along, to test my faith in fate once again.

And what came along was quite remarkable.

He was an old Indian. No, not a "Native American." He laughed at such PC phraseology. "White man's guilt," he called it and chuckled behind broken teeth. His face was deep mahogany-brown, his skin as wrinkled and weathered and tough as rhino hide, and his smile bright enough to illuminate a football stadium.

It was the smile that made me stop the camper and walk over to meet him. He was sitting near the side of the track on a large boulder, dressed in worn jeans, a big woolen sweater, and a purple bandanna over which his gray, wiry hair fell guru-like in matted tresses down to his shoulder blades.

I think I saw his smile before I really saw him. Maybe a trickle of sunlight caught his teeth. Who knows. But first came that great grin and then came Bill.

Bill! I was disappointed by his name, hoping for Eagle-Rising or Catch-Bear-for-Breakfast or Coyote-Calling or something a bit more Indianlike. But Bill it was and Bill it remained. He said he was some sub-tribe of Cherokee I'd never heard of. He pointed up through the trees to a cabin perched high atop a rock outcrop on the ridgeline of the mountain. He asked if I was thirsty. I wasn't but I said I was, so he led the way slowly up through the thick undergrowth between towering pines to his lonely aerie.

The vistas were incredible. All the way south down endless serrated ranges. The receding lines of hills blurred into warm blue mists. Two bald eagles soared on spirals, barely moving their wings—just gliding in great upward circles of flight.

He offered me water and then boiled up some concoction on an outdoor stove. He called it "tea" but it was unlike any tea I've ever drunk before or since. At first it seemed insipid—rather like the barely flavored hot water you get in the more mediocre of Chinese restaurants. But as I continued to sip from the mug slowly, watching the eagles, enjoying the amazing views and peering down into shadowy valleys and canyons, something began to work its magic. I felt increasingly thirsty and the more I drank of the tea the more its flavor expanded into a spectral array of tastes, from the tartest of lemons to the sweetest of sweets I've ever experienced. Its aroma was of lavender, rose petals, and peaches; its taste was more complex but somewhere in the mix seemed raisins, oranges, honey, and mint. The rest was indefinable. But it was wonderful and I felt wonderful and Bill just sat there sipping and grinning and grinning and sipping.

Our silence was full of fellowship. It seemed to go on for hours. No talk. Just tea-sipping and gazing. No mind-yammer either for a change. Just each moment. Perfect, whole, and complete in itself.

Eventually there was conversation of a kind. He talked of the mountains, of a tribal powwow he'd attended (no whites invited) a week or so ago, of the songs and the chantings that had stretched on through whole days and nights.

I asked him if he could sing one or two of the songs. He grinned as if he knew that's precisely what I'd ask and began by beating a stick in the dust at his feet, making a soft puckering kind of sound like distant drums, drums heard far away somewhere deep in the heart of the forest.

The sound and rhythm were hypnotic. At first it was a simple beat but as he continued it seemed to develop subtle counter-rhythms and a backbeat and the foot-shuffle hiss of flesh on soft sand (with my eyes closed it really sounded like scores of feet, all shuffle-dancing together).

And slowly he began to sing. Long plaintive lines, initially minor variations on a drone, in a deep monotone, but gradually expanding into higher registers, becoming plaintive, then stern and proud, then whispery, then sadly plaintive again as if beseeching something, asking for some special favor, for grace and generosity from...what?...the power of the earth, the sky? I wasn't sure. At least, not until much later.

But it was enough just to listen without having to "understand." Bill's face was lifted up toward the sun. The golden light of early evening etched the leathery puckers of his cheeks and gave the creases deep glowing shadows. His eyes were closed. Sometimes he was grinning, exuding utter happiness. Other times, in the softer plaintive passages, his face was devoid of expression as if he were opening himself up wide to receive whatever favors were to be bestowed upon him.

The faintest of breezes blew across the ridge, nudging fallen leaves and cooling us as we sat together, me with my tea and Bill with his songs and his tapping stick. And if I listened, really listened, I could hear the echoes of other voices, voices in unison, in a kind of earthy harmony, a harmony resonant with the earth and all the mysteries and powers and wonders contained within the earth.

Later, much later, I asked Bill if he could tell me what one of the songs meant—a particularly beautiful song with a fluid melodic line and a note at the end of some of the lines that was like no other note I'd ever heard—a quartertone, like the songs I'd heard so often in Iran? Or something else, a note not capable of placement on a page of written music. It was eerie and beautiful and seemed to have the ability to hang almost tangibly in the air long after he had moved on to other song lines.

"The words are simple," he said and grinned and I knew he didn't believe that at all. And I knew that they expressed the soul and spirit of ancient cultures, now almost destroyed and lost. And I knew—just by the sound of the music and those elusive grace notes—that they reflected a total, all-encompassing understanding of the way of all life—of a world in which man exists in harmony with all living and inanimate things and is part of the natural timeless rhythm which shapes and nurtures his environment and his whole existence. These songs were not contrived for idle amusement and entertainment, neither were they sung for the benefit of a few discerning listeners. For thousands upon thousands of years (just pause and think of that, particularly in relation to our own neophyte American culture barely a couple of centuries old) they were part of the tribal fabric, the melding force of ancient peoples, full of meaning, power, and deep spiritual resonance—direct communications with the infinite.

I was an eager student and I think Bill could sense that. I asked him to tell me the words of some of his songs. He smiled, nodded as if he knew I'd ask that too and began with the shortest of songs—the haikulike "Eagle's Song" (three simple lines, repeated and repeated):

The sun's rays
Lie along my wings
And stretch beyond their tips

Then he again sang the "Corn Song":

The corn grows up
The waters of the dark clouds drop, drop.
The rain descends.
The waters from the corn leaves drop, drop.
The rain descends.
The waters from the plains, drop, drop.
The corn grows up.
The waters of the dark mists drop, drop.

And then "The Rock":

Unmoved
From time without end,
You rest in the midst of the coming winds,
In the winds
You rest, aged one.
Small grasses grow around you
You are covered with the droppings of the birds,
Your top decked with downy feathers.
Oh, aged one.

Then another short haiku:

I am simply on the earth
Need I be afraid?

And then the most beautiful song of all, "The Mountain Chant," the one with those strange plaintive notes:

In beauty may I walk.
All day long may I walk.
Through the returning seasons may I walk.
On the trail marked with pollen may I walk.
With grasshoppers about my feet may I walk.
With dew about my feet may I walk.
With beauty may I walk.

And finally he sang the most powerful short-song of all again, chanted endlessly—"The Ghost Dance":

We shall live again.
We shall live again.

Evening was creeping in quickly now over the purpling ridges and I realized that I had to find my way out of the mountains on that elusive back road before dark.

I thanked Bill for his kindness and his company and then asked a question that I hadn't intended to ask. It just sort of appeared: "That last song. 'The Ghost Dance.' 'We shall live again.' Do you really believe that?"

Once again that grin. All-enveloping. All-embracing. "Yes," Bill replied simply, grinning that grin.

"But how?" I asked. "When so few Indians—so few of you—are left?"

Bill didn't respond to that one. He just grinned wider than ever—looked right into my eyes, deeper, deeper than anyone had looked before, and something inside me suddenly opened up—like a box, long locked and now unlocked. And I felt—I truly felt—as if he'd placed not only all the songs he'd sung for me into that box but the spirit behind the songs, the oh-so-ancient, oh-so-timeless knowledge that gave those songs their all-encompassing life and power.

And as I walked down the path from his tiny ridge-top cabin I felt myself filled with enormous richness and energy and vitality and the words of the "Ghost Dance" seemed to surround me and permeate every particle of my being. I heard the words as clearly as if Bill were singing them beside me. And I heard something else. I heard Bill's voice inside me saying, "We shall live again....We shall live again."

And I knew how too.

I celebrate myself, and sing myself...
For every atom belonging to me
As good belongs to you.
—WALT WHITMAN

Into the Vine

*How old are you? You look so incredibly ancient, curling
and twisting with your knotted limbs and veined branches...and so alive, rising in magnificent tangled torment
from this hard rocky earth. The earth of a Japanese garden
in a small city no one's ever heard of (even in Japan!), on
an island that's far away from the rest of this freeway-
networked and bullet train-laced nation.*

*What have you seen? What have you known? There
are ancient castle walls towering above you, dating back
to at least the twelfth century, so they say. Huge moss-
sheened slabs of rectangular granite, rough-shaped, like
you, not prissied up for decoration. These walls are tough
and enduring—like you. They have withstood armed
onslaughts and storms and even the great typhoons and
tsunamis that strike this part of the coast every once in a
while. And so have you, you splendid writhing creature.
You enduring, sinewy chaos of determination, with a
strength that seems to move directly into me as I sit down
on these boulders and pull out my sketch pad.*

I'm sketching you now. I'm looking into you. I'm feeling the power and the energy that is you and has been you for centuries. And I feel small and insignificant compared to you and yet I feel your power and energy too and the more I sketch you and try to capture the essence of what you are, the more I sense your power and energy moving into me and it makes my hand stronger, my line bolder, faster—flowing like the lines of your twisting torso as I move, deeper and deeper, into you....

Lost in the Bungle-Bungle

*Remote, mysterious, unknown places still exist
in our world—and, of course, within us all.*

Deep in the northwestern Outback of Australia I explored one of the oddest, and most evocative, landscapes known to man— the hidden miniworld of the Bungle-Bungle. Eroded down over hundreds of thousands of years from a vast sandstone plateau, Purnululu (to give it the Aboriginal name), consists of hundreds of stratified beehive-shaped hills each rising as high as 300 feet vertically from the vast ochre-colored desert. And here was yet one more invitation into the delights and infinite dimensions of the multi-self.

⌒

The wonders of this strange, sometimes eerie place have merged in my memory. Recollections return in drops and sprinklings of color, form, shape, and sound. To be alone in these strange clefts and canyons made me rejoice once again in the stroking comforts of solitude. I could imagine—I did imagine—that I'd discovered this place, just come across it on some long Outback odyssey, entered its passages and learned its secrets after days on the bright, brittle plains.

The Bungle took me in and enveloped me. For hours I sat in the shade of canyon walls, three or four hundred feet high, listening to the soft prattle of palm fronds, watching the shadows move with the sun across the smooth striped and tiered walls, rejoicing in the occasional cool breezes that wafted down from the high narrower places, letting the soft red sand on the floor of the canyons trickle through my fingers.

I drank from clear cold pools fed by secret springs; I shared a sandwich lunch with a pink-crested cockatoo; I watched tiny lizards scurry through the sharp, spiky grasses; I looked for Aborigine wall markings and symbols, but saw none. Even they, I later learned, were reluctant to wander within these mazelike clefts. They buried their dead here and left them in peace, among the timeless silences.

I remember particularly the grand climax to an arduous walk and climb through Cathedral Gorge, where, after squeezing at one point through a cleft no more than two feet wide, I finally entered a bowl shaded by an enormous rock archway in which I found a crystal pool fed by a trickling waterfall. The place echoed like the Blue Mosque in Istanbul, wispy threads of sound rolling around the towering curved walls.

I sat on a low dome of blown sand waiting for something to happen. Everything seemed set for an appearance, a celebration, an offering—something to give focus to a setting so spiritual, so silent, so majestic, that it's hard to believe it really existed.

To think such a place as this has gone untouched, unmolested, unexplored for so many millions of years without even

THE
BUNGLE-
BUNGLE
— Northwest
Australia

the modest intrusions of the Aborigines, gave new life to all my lost world explorations and expectations. There may be hundreds of such places, still unknown, still unmapped in our seemingly poor, cluttered, overdiscovered, overused world. Not "may." I know there are. Some are too small or fragile to mention, even to friends. Others are so remote and inaccessible that they exist in their wholeness, safe maybe forever from prying eyes and inquisitive minds. Vast underground worlds of water and caves and galleries dripping with millions of stalactites; deep, jungle-hidden grottoes harboring life forms as yet unknown and unrecorded; other canyons, other Bungle-Bungles, so elusive that we may never find them and never experience their beauty and their own special solitudes.

To know that our world still remains a thing of mystery, silence, and secrets—this I find one of the greatest joys of all. It gives me that shiver of pure *duende* that scampers through my body when I experience a place or a thing with new eyes and new sensations; when the mind's constant gauging, measuring, comparing, and contrasting cease and you gaze—mindless—at something so unexpected and so overwhelmingly all-encompassing that you're drenched in golden cascades of pure feeling. A great cleansing of the spirit, a breaking of barriers, an annihilation of "attitudes"—a powerful rush, upward and outward into infinite new possibilities, infinite new delights. A rejoicing in the great "I AM" and—even more—a reinforcement of the "you are," a sense of being propelled into far broader spaces and conceptions, and, most strange of all, a sense of coming home to a place that, somehow, deep, deep down, you always knew was there.

The real voyage of discovery consists not in seeking new landscapes, but in having new eyes.
—MARCEL PROUST

The Hunt

Sometimes you need to probe elemental
experiences to unleash elemental selves.

I was staying for a while with a Norwegian friend in a beauti-ful—unbelievably beautiful—fjord not far from his palatial ancestral home (apparently his family descended from some ancient king of Denmark who once conquered and ruled this part of Norway).

We had spent a few glorious days sailing out among the islands beyond the wide mouth of the fjord and learned much of the lore and enduring heritage of those lovely, lonely places.

On our return to the fjord we were toasting our fine adven-ture together with the local firewater, a knock-your-kneecaps-off version of the universal *eau de vie* or grappa or whatever countless names they give the stuff made from all that ultra-fermented (a.k.a. rotten and rancid) stuff left over when all the good stuff has gone into making the finer stuff—wines, brandies, and the like.

And we were happy. Partly due to the firewater but more so because we'd taken time to explore these almost-secret islands without haste. We'd also allowed each other glimpses behind the screens of our normal, everyday facades and probed gently, past lowered defenses, acknowledging our joint vulnerabilities, into the realm of our other, far less public selves, some not altogether familiar to either of us.

So it had been a kind of double-exploration journey, inner and outer, which is by far the most rewarding kind, and our friendship had grown as we had grown, together, with no pretenses and no cop-outs.

"I've got a little surprise for you tomorrow," said Michael, his face glowing with his "I-know-something-you-don't-know" grin.

"What, what!?" I exclaimed, like a kid wanting his present now.

"We're going hunting."

My insides immediately went gnarly and I didn't know what to say. I'd hunted only once before, and very reluctantly, when I lived in Iran, and I found it a very confusing and traumatic experience.

He assumed I hadn't heard him.

"I said—we're going hunting! Some of the villagers have a hunting club and they've invited us to join them on one of their deer hunts. They're not allowed many kills during the season so this is special. I thought you'd like to go."

"Fine. Yes. I'll go." I couldn't think of anything else to say (I'm a good guest. I go along.)

"It'll be great," gushed Michael. "We won't be hunting ourselves. We're not in their club so its illegal. So we go as honored guests—as observers."

"O.K. Great. That should be interesting. Thanks, Mike, for organizing it." I really did try to be enthusiastic but my heart wasn't in it, and after the times we'd just spent together, he knew that too.

"It'll be O.K. Dave. You'll learn a lot. Maybe give you an idea or two for an article."

Well, Mike, you were right. But I don't think this is the kind of article you had in mind. It's really a journal (and I used my old notebooks, with all the scraggly writing and blobs and rain and mud and extremely unshapely English) about how a group of men with a single purpose moved through a remarkable array of "selves" in one long day from 7 A.M. until dawn the following day.

Well—you might say, what's so interesting about that? Happens all the time—right? We all go through numerous moods and shape-shifts every day almost without thinking. And I guess you'd be right in a way. But read on. There's something deeper.

⁊

7:00 A.M. Out at the edge of the fjord. Chilly. Sun's behind the soaring cliffs. Hunters in camouflage getups, big leather boots, looking very hunter-like but acting like schoolkids on a day-trip. Pecking and pinching their wives, who are cooking up a storm of a breakfast in addition to all the usual cold cuts and fish platters (endless variations on the pickled herring theme) and hugging and rolling around in the grass with their kids. Lovely picture. Doesn't feel like a killing spree at all.

8:00 A.M. Wives and kids gone. Different mood now. Very macho. Almost immediately—like someone flicked a switch. Stern faces, gun-checking, leader showing pincer-movement strategy on a map to the twelve men to drive deer up to the steepest slopes of the fjord. A somber toast (more of that ghastly *eau de vie*), even Mike is somber now. A spirit of team resolution. Each for all. And then they're gone.

8:30 A.M. Mike and I are taken up a "back way" track in a jeep with our guide to a rock overlook. Great spot. Sun coming up now. Fantastic fall colors. Distant vistas and fjord. Mood of deep silence and utter peace. I could build a home here.

9:30 A.M. Still no sign of hunters. They have a long climb. Mosquitoes nibbling now. Told to be absolutely still by our guide. Tried, but I'm not much good at that kind of thing. Too restless. Too full of conflicting emotions.

10:15 A.M. Finally—I see two of the hunters. Way, way down in a forest clearing. Still no sounds. Amazing how quiet twelve big strapping men can be.

10:35 A.M. Sudden noise in the forest—cracking and crunching. Then silence. All very still. It's getting hot now. Desperately want to take my parka off. Guides gives a menacing "no-way" sign.

And then suddenly—it's there in the clearing just below our rock. Just a scamper away. Massive. Fawn coat, large antlers, white underbelly. And wary. Sniffing the air. Know's something's not right. Turns head slowly, still sniffing. Hunters are downwind, so should be no human odors. But it knows...it knows....

A single shot—incredible jarring sound after two hours of utter stillness. Deer turns. The hunter missed? Then it stumbles onto its knees, its back legs still strong and upright. Then—like someone pushed—just falls over on its side, breathing heavily. Men tearing up the slope out of the forest. We hurl ourselves down from the rock and gather around the dying deer. Someone wants to perform the *coup de grâce* with another shot. The leader says a gentle, "No. She's gone."

And I watch and we all watch as the life ebbs tangibly out of the creature. And then finally out of the eyes—oh those wondrous, beautiful eyes. I have never seen such a brilliant sapphire blue. Luminous. Shining from within, then slowly, slowly the color fades, into a deep green-gray. No one moves. They must have witnessed this many times before but everyone is transfixed by those eyes. Two men are obviously moved and lower their heads. I am almost weeping. And Michael too. Even the leader looks touched by it all. More long silence. Then there's an abrupt: "O.K. Cut. Save the meat. Quick." (Apparently there's some gland that has to be removed fast or the meat turns rancid, even poisonous.)

This bit I can't watch. Three men vanish again into the forest. Maybe too much for them too?

Mike and I are a bit morose. The deer is rapidly and skillfully skinned and divided into big portions, placed in plastic bags and the men make ready to leave.

Then another shot in the forest. Everyone stiffens. The leader bows his head. And then comes the real sadness. The three men return dragging a tiny dead fawn behind them into the clearing. The leader looks at my face. I feel suddenly angry and outraged. A little fawn!? What's the point of killing that for God's sake? He knows my thoughts.

"If we had left it behind it would have starved to death or been torn to pieces by wolves. This is—was—the mother (he pointed reluctantly to the bloody plastic bags)—we had to take them both..." Then he added quietly and unconvincingly, "It's the law."

11:15 A.M. Back in the camp by the fjord. No wives, no children, no celebration. Just a cold sandwich lunch. Some of the men are going back for more afternoon hunting. I've had enough. Everyone looks like they've got bad hangovers. I agree—reluctantly—to meet them all up at their "hunting lodge" way up near the top of the fjord cliffs around six in the evening for a "special dinner."

6:30 P.M. "The Special Dinner." My mood is a little better and improves with firewater. We share ritual raw slices of the deer's liver (unpleasant, but a local custom I guess). They toast the two deer (the afternoon crew shot nothing else). And they mean it. Their eyes speak of pride in the beauty and skill of those lovely creatures. In their hearts they're back in ancient times now with their ancestors when deer and other game and fish were all they had and fall hunts were vital to prepare for the long, harsh winters. They are their great-great-grandfathers now. They even speak differently—deeper, slower, more thoughtful, clearer, despite the thwack of that ghastly firewater.

8:00 P.M. Have to admit they cook a fantastic dinner. Roasted venison chateaubriand and other delicious parts (the remaining cuts have already been salted for curing and winter eating). Simple loganberry and other fruit sauces, potatoes (the staple, and oh so dull, like most Norwegian dishes), sour cream, and a mass of fresh fern fiddleheads poached in butter and beer.

9:15 P.M. The songs come. Long sad songs at first. The men show no embarrassment singing despite lousy voices. They're still with their ancestors, doing what they did.

And then the stories—the legends and myths told mainly by the leader, who is obviously a fine storyteller. The men are like kids, mesmerized, spreading capes on the floor, their chins cupped on their hands despite the fact that they know the words, forwards and backwards.

More booze flows. Songs get a bit more racy—tits and bums and the like. They're adolescents now, seared by the lusts of youth and the lure of young fjord maidens.

And then, one by one, they collapse on the wooden floor of the lodge and drift like babies, curled embryolike (yes, even one sucking his knuckles), into boozy sleep, punctuated by great flubberblasts of snoring.

5:00 A.M. First light of dawn and time for the long hike back down the mountains to their families, their homes, their responsible jobs (ties, suits, polished shoes, etc.), and their everyday lives. Their everyday selves.

And Michael is right. It has been indeed a fascinating experience. Even as a nonparticipant—an observer—I feel I've been bashed about and roller-coasted by emotions and conflicting feelings. And I count the number of men I've seen in a single day in each single man—at least a dozen—and doubtless many more I missed when they were deep in the forest. And these were more than just different moods. They were like entirely different people living in the same bodies.

I slept well that night and woke thinking what strange, contradictory, wonderful, endlessly fascinating and mysterious creatures we all are.

And I was very happy with that thought.

> *It is your destiny to play an*
> *infinity of creative roles.*
> —DEEPAK CHOPRA

The Blissful World of Hannah Hauxwell

*There's a lot to be gained from helping
strangers along the way.*

A few years back I explored the 270-mile-long Pennine Way up the "Backbone of England," the longest and possibly the finest of all Britain's long-distance footpaths. It provided a most revelatory series of experiences including this brief meeting with a woman who lived alone on a remote moorland farm.

 ✐

At the reservoir in Baldersdale I celebrated the Pennine Way halfway point with handfuls of ice-cold spring water and then—just as my ankle gave way for the third time that day after another tumble on the tussocks—I spotted a middle-aged woman in a tattered purple pullover and baggy black trousers held up by a loop of string. She stood with a shovel in a pile of manure. Her cheeks were holly-berry bright, and her hair, brilliantly silver, haloed her head.

"Tha's gone and hurt thissen, then? Come n'sit thissen down a bit, please," she said, indicating a tiny milking stool in the cow byre. "Just gi' us a minute. Bessie's got all excited and made messies. I'm a bit particular and I 'ate walkin' in clarts. If there's one clart about tha' carries it around all day."

She cleaned up meticulously and let me into her dark farmhouse where she told me she'd lived alone since her mother's death in 1958. The kitchen was crammed with cardboard boxes piled halfway to the ceiling, and it was only later that I found out what they all contained. We huddled around a tiny electric heater and she served me glasses of fresh milk while her Jack Russell terrier, Tim, pranced around trying to get a sip.

She told me about her love for her little valley. "I don't get far but I don't need to. There's nothin' I like better than goin' through that iron gate and down t' trees and water. That little stream by t' first bridge. I go there a lot."

We talked about her five cows. "I can't afford more but I enjoy what I have. They're just like people—some have a calm temperament, others are excitable, and a few can be downright bossy and nasty."

I wondered if she ever got lonely. "Oh never, never. I've so many things I want to do. There's the wallin', slatin', there's weedin', muckin' out. I'm going to make jam tomorrow. I used to make butter too. I can still hear that sound when it, what we call, 'broke'—a lovely slushin' sound as it got thicker. Oh no, I'll never catch up with miself. Some people free 'emselves up and then they've got lots of time and no idea what to do with it."

She noticed I was still limping. "I'm a great one for walkin' sticks," she said and vanished. Five minutes later she was back with a fresh-cut ash stick. "It's a clumsy brute," she apologized. "I'll just dress it up a bit to neaten it, please." I held it while she stripped the bark from the handle and tip with a pocketknife.

She seemed one of those people gifted with a natural earthy wisdom. "Success seems to me to be much more than just a lot of things lyin' round—there's as many ways of success as there are people."

And then she said something that has remained with me for years:

"Y'know living here like this, y'think a lot and y'see a lot. People stop by when they're walkin' the Way and d'y'know, I hardly say hello and give 'em a glass of milk before I feel I know 'em. Ah mean know 'em inside like. Everything about 'em—good, bad, sad, happy. And they've hardly opened their mouths! Now ain't that strange if you please!"

"How do you think you know them—so quickly, so well," I asked, already suspecting her answer.

"I dunno really. I suppose it's because they're already...like, inside me. Like I'm meeting parts of me I 'aven't met for quite a while. It's really nice...they're all old friends before they've hardly finished their milk!"

Very reluctantly I left her and limped up the long hill from the farm with my new stick. She stood waving all the time.

"Come back, please, if it hurts," was the last I heard.

Later than night the barmaid at The Rose and Crown pub in Mickleton told me I'd just spent the afternoon with Hannah Hauxwell, whose happy face had become the stuff of legends following a recent TV documentary on her life. And the cardboard boxes? "Oh, they're full of letters," she said, "from people all over the world. She's living in a house bursting with love."

Twilight at Kingley Vale

Hidden in a deep combe at the end of a mile-long track across cornfields northwest of Chichester is the Kingley Vale Nature Reserve. According to local legend, this sinister grove of yew trees changes its shape at night and wanders the valley together with the ghosts of Vikings defeated here in 874 A.D. by the local Saxons. The Anglo-Saxon Chronicle *records that the local citizens "put them to flight and killed many hundreds of them." Even on a bright summer afternoon the place has an eerie quality. The gnarled trees huddle in deep gloom at the base of the hill. The Nature Conservancy claims this to be one of Europe's finest yew forests. The ancient trees writhe silently under a canopy of exploding branches. Clematis, or "old man's beard," cascades in gray curtains, shrouding the grove and cutting out the light. Streamers of creeping plants dangle like snakes in a tropical rain forest. Close up the grain bursts through thin bark, swirled and contorted as if every inch of growth was agony and death was imminent. Branches lie broken and rotting on a brown carpet of needles. A single strand of sun*

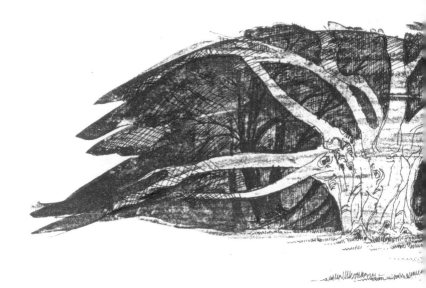

pierces the darkness and falls on a patch of spongelike moss. Drops of dew sparkle, and the dampness of moist decay hangs thick in the grove. It's a magical place that stays in the mind.

And something happened to me here. Something very strange.

In the rather foreboding gloom of the vale, I saw a figure about fifty feet away walking slowly towards me as I walked slowly towards him. We were dressed in the same clothes, carrying the same sticks, with the same sweat-matted hair. I stopped and looked closely. We were quite close now. And it was me. Just the same. But somehow different. Whether it was a trick of light or a reflection conjured up in a tangle of spiderwebs, or—whatever, I have no idea. The figure I looked at seemed younger, full of energy, glowing a little in the gloom and utterly—blissfully—happy. An aura

of pure spiritual radiance surrounded the figure—I felt it touch me, move inside and warm me like a sudden blast of brandy, from the tips of my toes to the top of my head. My body buzzed with vigor, and waves of euphoria I have known only rarely in my life rippled through me as if I were a beach being lapped by a gentle surf. I felt dizzy—wonderfully, weightlessly dizzy—so light I sensed, for a few seconds, that I was actually floating.

And then it was over and the vale was dark again and the yews were reaching out with their menacing arms.

But the memory, the actuality, of that euphoria, that all-encompassing sense of well-being and joy and excitement, has never left, and at times, when life becomes a little oppressive, I can reach into myself and release a little of that magic, the magic of the reflected self, the magic that lies deep within all of us.

White Water Wisdom—The River Within

*Our outer worlds and inner worlds are
more similar than we think.*

Bus travel seems endless. People get on, people get off, but the journey goes on forever. The only thing that changed on this trip were the occupants of the seat beside me. So far I'd had three Indian companions, each of whom had slept through all the noise, heat, and confusion. I envied them their tranquility.

And then Dick Davies appeared, a young Welshman with a prematurely old face, deeply lined and flecked with dark scars. He wore an old suede hat, Australian style, with one brim turned up, baggy green corduroys, and a torn leather jacket so stained with grease and mud it was difficult to tell its original color.

At first I thought that he, too, would sleep out the journey, but our conversation became animated when we compared notes on Kathmandu and the Himalayas.

"I'm a real white-water nut," he told me with a grin that made his old face suddenly look very young. "Himalayas, Central America, New Zealand, Africa, you name it. I've been kayaking there."

He was a true world wanderer, who had spent much of the last decade of his life seeking out white-water wonderlands all around the globe. I felt a little envious as I often do when listening to other travelers' tales.

"I've never done any white-water stuff," I said. "Somehow I don't think I'd enjoy it that much."

He laughed. "It doesn't make much difference what you do really. Like anything good in life, you end up pretty much in the same place."

"And you get there by kayaking."

"Yeah. Listen, I'm not one of the religious types. Y'know. You've met them. Nepal, Ladakh, the south. They're all over India. They're all looking for something that makes everything make sense."

"Centering?"

"Centering? O.K.—that's your word. Call it anything you want. It's all the same. You know what it is when you get there."

"And kayaking. That's what you do."

"Yeah. But it could be something else—anything."

The driver had finally turned off the raucous tape, which he'd played over and over since our departure. It was really hot now despite the breezes through the open windows of the bus. Everyone seemed to be asleep.

"What's it like? Kayaking."

Dick smiled and sighed. "It's a bit of everything. It's good some days, lousy other times. Like life. You take a knock and you get up and you go again. But each time, it's better. You learn to trust. You learn to trust yourself, and you learn to trust the water. You never fight her, try to beat her. She'll always win. You've got to read her right—understand her."

"And how do you do that?"

"Hard work, boyo! You walk each set of the rapids first."

"Walk?"

"On the edge, on the boulders. Try to see the next one and the one after that. Try to see it all, find out where the rocks are, how wide the chutes, where the keeper waves are—they can be rough—they go backwards and they'll spin you like a top, like a bloody blender. If there's rocks underneath, you can bust your legs—chop, chop, chop—smash 'em to pieces. It's those that don't do their homework that never get back to brag about it."

"But what's it really like? When you're actually in there heading for the rapids?"

"Lousy. Like you're going to piss in your pants—or worse."

"Every time?"

"Almost. Sometimes it happens too fast and you don't have time to think what you're thinking. You trust your memory—and your instincts. You've never got time to make second decisions. If it's a string of rapids—those are the best—and you come out wrong from the first one, well, you've just got to improvise. That's when you need all your instincts—and balls of brass! All the stuff you've ever learned. One paddle wrong and the bloody thing can be upside down in a twinkling and then you've got problems. A whirlie'll get you sure as mustard if you're not ready for it. You get in a hole, under a rock, and you're there forever!"

"Is this what you tell people?"

"Hell—that's just the start!" He paused and lit one of

those noxious little Nepalese cigarettes. "You've got no idea. You've always got to be ready for anything. Stopper rocks—they flip you, and they're hard to miss if you don't get enough of a warning. Then there's haystacks, souses, satins, eddies, fillies, and spinners. If you hit them wrong they'll send you twisting all over the shop, right into an eye or something."

"What's an eye?"

"You'll only get to look into a good one once. When you're being sucked in, round and round, like on the inside of an ice-cream cone. And there's the eye—that black eye—right at the bottom. If you get that close it's bye-bye baby, bye-bye."

"You do this kind of kayaking often?"

"Often as I can."

I knew I was going to ask him. And I did. "Why this? Why not something a bit safer?"

"Hell, if I knew the answer to that one—"

"You get a high or something? Adrenaline?"

"Yeah, yeah. You get high. Later. But when you're in it—I don't know—it's hard to say what it is. But it gets into you. Even if you don't do it for weeks or months. There was a year once I never went near white water. My legs were shot. One broken in two places, the other mangled up below the knee. But I knew I'd be back. Once you've done it for a while, and once you get the hang of it—" He paused and sucked on his tiny cigarette. "You're alive. I'm not kidding. You're so alive you could bust a nut. I don't get that feeling from anything else. Not even in bed, y'know. Doesn't matter who I'm with. I never get it like I get it on a ride—when you're heading for that edge, right after the riffs, and—even if you've done your homework—you still don't know, there's no way you can tell what the hell's gonna happen next, except that you're going down, you're going over the drop, down the chute, and you're not going to finish until you're finished—or until she's finished with you."

"Why 'she'? Why not 'it'?"

"Oh, it's a bloody 'it' sometimes. Most times it's an 'it.' You curse the bastard. But like I said, she gets you, she gets into you, and you can't stop going back. And when the ride's over, when you get to the back end and she's calmed out and you're floating around feeling great and dead cocky well—you know, she just feels like a woman."

"Like she knows what you've done."

"Yeah. Yeah, something like it. Like she knows what you've done. Like you're O.K. You got through again."

"And that you'll be back."

"Oh yeah. Hell, yeah. She knows you'll be back. Just like a woman knows."

We both sat quietly for a while. Something he'd said brought back a memory.

"Y'know, I almost drowned when I was a kid," I said. "Near a waterfall. I fell under and couldn't get back up. I'm sure that stupid experience put me off the idea of messing around on white water."

"Oh yeah. Well—that'll do it."

"You never got close to drowning?"

He nodded but didn't seem to want to talk about it. The smoke from his cigarette curled around his hat.

"One time I think I did drown." He spoke slowly.

"Meaning?"

"Well, I don't really know. Something strange. Still don't know what happened."

I knew he wanted to tell me so I just waited. He lit another cigarette.

"Hell—it was a long time back. When I first got started. I'd only been doing it a few weeks. And I was lousy. I mean lousy. Couldn't get the hang of it. I wanted to, but I couldn't. It wouldn't come right. Anyway, this one day I was up in Scotland by myself, the Cairngorms, trying to get it right, and every-thing's going O.K. until, zoot! I was under the boat and then out of it and I couldn't touch the bottom and I didn't know where the hell I was. And jeez, was it cold! Real brass monkey stuff and churning away like mad. Currents all over the place, and I was flippin' over like a hooked fish. I'd sucked in a lot of water, I couldn't find the surface. It was black as pitch. I'd got no air left. I knew I was drowning. And all these weird things were happening. You get flashbacks like they tell you—like I was crying because I'd broken one of my mother's best plates. Then I was on a soccer pitch with the mates. All kinds of stuff. Coming home down the lane from church past the pub and hearing them all singing and then it all sort of went quiet and it wasn't like I was in water or anything, it was just O.K. and there didn't seem to be much to worry about anymore."

His cigarette trembled in his fingers. The afternoon sun flickered through a filigree of stunted tree branches along the roadside.

"And then, well everything got weird. I wasn't in the water. I was on the bank, lying on some sand, and the boat was right by me and it looked fine and I felt fine. I wasn't even coughing or anything."

He shook his head and grinned. "Hell—I dunno what happened. Still don't. I thought I'd drowned, lost it. Into the great yonder and all that. Weird. I don't know how the hell I got to be sprawling like a Sunday afternoon fisherman on a riverbank with the boat and everything—all together in one piece."

My spine was tingling. That was my story from the bridge in Iran. The accident that hadn't happened. One of the half dozen or so strange events that changed my life and my way of looking at life entirely.

We sat quietly for a long time listening to the hiccupy rhythm of the bus engine.

"So that didn't put you off going back in?"

"Nope—I've been kayaking ever since. I learned fast after that. Seemed to come naturally."

"And you don't get scared about drowning?"

"No. Never thought about it since that first time. I've been banged about a bit y'know. But that's all part of the game. But no. No, I don't think about drowning."

"She must have liked you a lot."

He laughed. "Yeah. Yeah she must. She still does!"

"Like a lover," I said but didn't know why I said it. I was just looking at his face—at a face that, despite all his horrendous experiences—glowed, well, like a man in love.

It was his turn to look at me now. Long and deeply.

"Can you *see* that? Is that what you *see*?" he asked finally, almost desperately.

"Yes."

"Shoot!" He swallowed hard and sat silently for a while.

"Y'know," he continued, "no one's ever seen that, or at least no one's ever *said* it!"

"Long bus journeys can do that. You've got hours to kill. You meet a stranger, someone like you—who you'll never see again more than likely. And you take risks. It's like being anonymous. You see things you possibly wouldn't normally see and you say things you wouldn't normally say."

"Yeah. You're right there."

He seemed deep in thought again. Then finally he leaned over a little closer.

"If I say something a bit stupid, will you forget it?"

"Sure," I said (but obviously, I didn't, so it wasn't).

He took a deep breath.

"There is a *she* in my rivers. And I am, as you said, in love with her in a weird kind of way. And the rivers...the rivers I ride are *in me*. It's like I'm living on different levels—in different realities—all at the same time. They're outside of course in one way, but they're inside me too. Sometimes so much so that I don't always know where I end and the river...she...begins. Sometimes there seem to be no boundaries...like it's all merged into one thing...a river within..."

"Yes," I said. "I think I know what you mean."

He turned and laughed—really laughed for the first time on this crazy bus journey—and all the scowls and angst vanished from his face.

"Yeah—I do believe you do know, mate. I *really* do believe you do."

"Come to the edge," he said.
They said, *"We are afraid."*
"Come to the edge," he said.
They came.
He pushed them...
And they flew.
—GUILLAUME APOLLINAIRE

The Peacock's Tail —A Journey in Solitude

Sometimes you need to truly let go to reach the deeper reality of the present moment.

Thankfully there were no "hard bits" for the first few miles. I felt as if I were walking on soft clouds across the bouncy buttongrass path that headed southeast from Melaleuca toward Cox Bight, my first destination on this seven-day odyssey on Tasmania's infamous—but utterly majestic—South Coast Path. No roads, no settlements, no supplies and, more than likely, no people at this time of the year—for a whole week. There are few treks in Australia—or for that matter, in the world—as lonely or arduous as this one and I set out with no small amount of trepidation.

It was couple of hours before the silence began to creep in and I realized that seven days of solitude suddenly seemed like a hell of a long time. On most of my long-distance hikes I've usually had company for at least part of the journey. But on this one I had no one and no real prospect of hearing a human voice unless I met someone coming the other way. What should I do with all that time? Dictate some short stories into my tape recorder? Start my autobiography? Compose a few songs? Compress all my world-wanderer realizations into a few pungent anagrams? Or merely go mad, howling at this desolate unpeopled place like a hyped-up hyena?

Goethe got it right, as he usually did: *In every parting there is a latent germ of madness.* Or Father Navarette: *It is no small contradiction to human nature to leave one's home.* Well—home was a long way off, just about as far as it could be on any part of the globe. But the balance will come, I told myself. It always does. In any situation, a benign reality usually composes itself out of the oddest of circumstances. Just let it come in its own time. Let the journey take on its own rhythm and pace and flow. Celebrate this unexpected spill of free days and then just flow with it.

The path stuck to the plain at first, which narrowed gradually between the misty New Harbour and Bathurst Ranges. Mount Counsel, with its quartzite flanks, glowered down. My map showed an enticing place—Hidden Valley—high on its upper flanks and normally I'd be tempted to take such a diversion. But the land discouraged such fancies. I recognized this kind of country from my days back home among the Pennine bogs of Yorkshire. I knew how the seductively soft surface of the heath could give way without warning to a pernicious spongy substrata and mud holes that sucked and gurgled at unsuspecting limbs and devoured boots with malicious glee, leaving walkers in goo-laden socks while their footwear was absorbed forever into the acidic mulch of the mire. The hardy walkers who ignore such trails across territory like this are known in England as "bog-trotters" as they leap like over-sized, overweight ballet dancers from tussock to tussock. Some are lucky and escape the embarrassing boot-losing predicaments. Many do not and end up being half carried, half dragged off the stagnant plateaus, puddled in gobbets of black goo by their grinning colleagues to the warmth and nurture of valley pubs.

There were no pubs or inns, however, on this hike and I hadn't brought a spare pair of boots, only some soft sneakers for evenings by my campfires. If I lost my boots I wondered what I'd do—or, more precisely, what the trail would do—to my feet. Not to mention the leeches.

Here it starts, I thought. The old mind-yammer. The silly fantasy-plagued "what if" scenarios that can wear a buoyant spirit down to a morose depression in a few unchecked reveries. None of those on this trip, please. All I have is me this time.

I tried to lift my confidence with memories of other solo journeys: that trek through Panama's Darien; those days on the deserted beaches of my "secret" island; my unsuccessful but still memorable climb up Central Africa's Ruwenzori range. They all began this way—a little wobbly at first as the spirit finds the fine line between freewheeling fantasy and the darker deeps of the mind—and then on into the days of balance and balm when the experience becomes pure, clean adventure.

≈

Dawn was promising enough, a crystal-clean light pushing the night clouds out to sea and touching the land with gold. No rain, no winds. A fine day for walking. The surly Ironbounds rose up in front of me, gilded peaks with jagged summits and flecks of ice and snow on the ridges. An ancient bulwark of Precambrian metamorphic rocks. Very impressive.

A majestic bird flew overhead as I collapsed the tent and loaded the backpack. Its large white head was hawklike and its white belly sparkled as it soared the updrafts with a broad wingspan of five feet or more. I learned later I'd seen a sea eagle, a voracious eater of reptiles, other birds and, when available, even penguins. Not a very pleasant creature—but on that sparkling morning it seemed an omen of better days ahead.

The path climbed steadily up open sedgeland into a broad subalpine zone. Pockets of King Billy pine clustered in gullies and sheltered places, their deeply furrowed trunks and branches contorted, juniper-fashion. Small white daisies with golden centers glowed in the wind-scoured scrub; compact clusters of dainty red Christmas bells rose among the grasses.

In spite of their ominous name, the Ironbounds peak at little more than three thousand feet, and while the climbing was tough going, it was made easier by the benign weather and ever broadening vistas of mountains and bays. I strode the skyline on razored ridges. The wind increased as I approached the summit and I spotted places where previous walkers had camped, huddled in the low bushes. I considered calling an early halt to the day and hunkering down to enjoy the views, but my legs kept on moving and I followed the contours around the northern rim of the massif, humming happy songs and wondering how to prepare a celebratory feast of my one solitary steak for dinner that night.

✐

The morning broke luminous, cloudless. I saw new patterns of vegetation from these heights, patterns that were invisible at lower elevations—brilliant green swatches of sphagnum moss invading the small ponds and pools that lay scattered across the mosaics of darker green and bronze cushion-plant plains. The patterns were jigsawlike, thousands of micro-environments from the sedge grasses to the mosses to the lichen-blotched rocks and strata. Patches of pink mountain rocket and cheeseberry bushes adorned with bright red berries gave a rich resonance to the more muted tones of the button-grass plateaus.

On a dull day the colors would doubtless be leached out to an army-tent khaki, but today the sun revealed the land's true richness: a brilliant panoply of tones and textures that made me wish for canvas, palette, and brushes; a magnificent display of the subtleties, the intricate juxtapositions and meldings of plant colonies set beside the milky whorls and snakelike doodlings of sand patterns beneath the blue-green waters of the coastal bays.

And yet, despite all these delights, I could sense the restless riot of the land itself: towering broken cliffs; spars of brittle basalt; fjordlike incisions where the warmer, higher post-Ice Age waters had penetrated deep into once-forested valleys; bold bluffs and phallic intrusions of dolerite into the spuming surf; the bleedings of frost-shattered ridges and razored escarpments in the form of peat-brown streams pouring from the hills; the bleached bones of ancient bedrocks protruding through the sloozy-oozy mud; the wind-torn trunks of trees, blasted of bark, blanched and twisted by a tempestuous climate that just never lets up—scratching and scraping the land down to its ultimate peneplain in the howling vastness that is southwest Tasmania.

I had a sudden flash of the neat little hedge-rimmed fields, ordered orchards, and Ireland-green, sheep-studded vales that awaited me way to the east around Hobart, far beyond these tumultuous ranges. I thought of the curling country roads, the pie shops smelling of fresh-baked pastry, the rowdy, beer-swilling pubs, and the demure, tin-roofed bungalows adorned with red and white trim and set in gardens of privet, hollyhocks, and geraniums.

I would be there soon, I promised myself—showered, deloused, primed up on Foster's ale, choosing dinner from menus with fancy borders, sleeping on soft mattresses, dry and warm, and savoring all the wonders of a world that, up here, seemed very, very far away.

But enough of such hedonistic imaginings. I was less than halfway to such bucolic destinations, with a lot of tough hiking ahead and challenges to be overcome.

And the challenges came fast. Actually a mere hour or so after my contemplations on the Ironbound range, as I left the heights and began my descent toward the long beach on Prion Bay, everything changed. The bare, wind-tossed tops gave way to some of the thickest, most tangled and tortured rain forest it has ever been my misfortune to encounter. I was out of the bright light and into a gray-green gloom of a nefarious netherworld.

Now, rain forests have their fascinations. Even an eerie dwarf forest I'd discovered at Cox Bight possessed, in daylight, a certain rampant, raging charm. But this was altogether different—a far more intense, menacing place where there seemed to be little in the way of order or subtlety. The forest just flared up and thrust me into it, following a trail that had the remarkable ability to vanish in the difficult places, leaving me scrambling through mud and slime and decaying moss beds without any sense of direction—except down.

And down and down, deeper into the sticky gloom of ancient Gondwanaland species—more tall King Billy pines, eucalyptus, myrtles, celery-top pines, and a tangled understory of laurel, whitewood, waratah, dwarf beech, and ferns, all competing for scarce light and root space—oh, and those mosses too, in strange and exotic forms: pillars, mattresses, balls, bouquets, and furry smotherings of trunks and branches. Had the mood been more conducive I might have dallied here and undertaken a photographic essay of these myriad species, possibly even bagged a few samples for later identification. But the mood was definitely not conducive to anything except survival and eventual extrication to the beaches I could see far, far below.

I arrived a few hours later, tottering with tiredness, at the graceful arc of Deadman's Bay, enclosing yet another soft white sand beach. Most of the rain forest lay behind me but exuberant flurries of vegetation encroached on the shore and clustered thickly along either bank of Deadman's Creek. I was tempted to camp for the night but, as dusk was a way off and the sky still contained slivers of blue, I decided to continue on around Menzies Bluff to the four-mile linear strand of Prion Beach.

Then, unexpectedly—and certainly uninvited—as I walked the seemingly endless beach, a dark sense of loneliness and utter isolation descended on me. The place looked so empty. So untouched. Somehow its drama and beauty exaggerated the intensity of my strange mood. Surely I shouldn't feel depressed in the midst of such magnificent scenery. I should feel elated, full of a sense of achievement. After all I was now well over halfway home. Only another three days at most before the cozy comforts of Cockle Creek.

But the mood wouldn't lift. I felt as buckled as an old worn belt. The beach seemed to go on forever. No footprints. No signs of campsites. Nothing—except me and this enormous, awesome space.

Something seemed to be banging against the edges of my mind. Am I being punished? Is this some kind of comeuppance? I remembered a quote from James Hillman: "The way through the world is more difficult to find than the way beyond it." I sensed I had reached an impasse of sorts. My expectations of this experience did not correspond with the actuality. And what made it so odd was that, as soon as that impasse occurred, I began hunting in my head for a rationale, a definition of my "problem"—my unexpected depression, tottering on the slimy abyss of self-doubt. *What's happening?* my mind called out. This is not the way it's supposed to be. But something on the other side, a whisper, a mere breath of thought, came through: There's no "meant to be," there's only "is." And a memory. A memory of lines from Thomas Moore's splendid book, *Care of the Soul* (I found the quotation later):

> Modern psychology...is often seen as a way of being saved from the very messes that most deeply mark human life as human. We want to sidestep negative moods and emotions, bad life choices, and unhealthy habits. But if our purpose is first to observe the soul as it is, then we may have to discard the salvational wish and find deeper respect for what is actually there. By trying to avoid human mistakes and failures, we move beyond the reach of the soul.

And later—at the end of Moore's book:

> We know soul is being cared for when our pleasures [in my case the opposite, but the point's the same] feel deeper than usual, when we can let go of the need to be free of complexity and confusion, and when compassion takes the place of distrust and fear.

It is the "letting go" that is the key. The releasing of expectations and predigested experiences and the acceptance of "what is"—good, bad, elating, depressing, hurtful, ecstatic—all the myriad range of emotions and feelings and insights that have always been and always will be a part of our mutual human fabric. (As a friend once told me with great "got it" glee: "Y'see, this freedom thing is all a matter of seeing stumbling blocks as stepping stones...")

Only then, according to Moore, does the soul coalesce "into the mysterious philosopher's stone, that rich, solid core of personality the alchemists sought, or it opens into the peacock's tail—a revelation of the soul's colors and a display of its dappled brilliance."

Moore's image of the peacock's tail had endured in my mind and it came at just the right moment. Something was happening. As I slowly began to accept the strange mood that had so abruptly swept over me, it no longer seemed to be a problem but merely another nuance, another facet, of the journey's multifaceted sequence. It didn't really matter much whether I felt sadness or gladness; the mood was irrelevant to the process—the learning, the insights, the new ways of seeing that were now somehow encompassing the depression and leading me on to another level of perception.

Something definitely was happening. Something I remembered from a Tom Robbins novel (I forgot which) that suggested the difference between an adventure and a suicide is that the adventurer leaves himself a margin of escape, and the narrower the margin, the greater the adventure. Well, I certainly hadn't come all this way for a lonely suicide in this desolate land; I'd come on an adventure, to narrow the margins, follow the escape routes, and see where they led.

And this one was leading to somewhere rather wonderful, a place an Aborigine had tried to explain to me a few weeks previously during my journeys in the wilds of western Australia. He talked of a web of song (the songlines) and legends that enveloped the world, a web in which time was irrelevant. Everything that is and ever was and will be is part of that web—everything in constant interaction—everything in kinship within the web—all humans, all creatures, all mountains, rivers and streams, trees, even individual rocks, all animate and interrelated within an all-enveloping web.

My walk was now no longer a morose, bad mood plod. In fact, I was now unaware of actually walking on this immense sandy strand. I was literally becoming "part of it"; the still silent place was buzzing with "presence"; the web was forming. The sheaves of dune grass, the fuzzy huddle of dwarf forest on the lee side of the dunes, the soft slitheriness of millions of sand grains, the tiny marks and footprints etched in the grains, the hiss and suck of the surf, the breezes swirling among the marram grass, the slowly undulating movements of the clouds, the fractured complexities of the distant dolerite crags—even the silence itself both in the land and, growing more each minute, in my mind...all part of the eternal web. A web which is another reality, where things are not fractured, fragmented, labeled, separated, but rather bound together in an inevitable totality that melts the barriers of insight, merges the boundaries between things, and lets the incredible wholeness and completeness of everything come roaring through into a previously blinkered, and now suddenly unlocked, perception.

All the clever doodads of the mind—rationales, expectation, critical faculties, intellectual framings, prejudices, fears, measurements, discretions, manners (you know all the rest)—seemed to drown in a deluge from some subconscious force that had lain dormant in me for too long and was now released with such vigor and clarity that "moods" seemed to be easily breachable barriers—even welcome doors—into the miracle of the *now,* the infinitely intricate web of a reality without time and without boundaries.

And so—back to my Tasmanian beach, my seemingly endless stretch of soft sand, glowing golden beneath clouds dainty as duck-down, where my bad mood was no longer even a memory and I gave myself up, for the first time on the journey, to the wholeness and wonder of the place itself. And my soul indeed slowly discovered its "peacock's tail," and, as it opened, and the colors revealed themselves, and all the amazing array of the me-s—the memories, the people, all the experiences that reflect other facets of the self—all this incredible kaleidoscopic array of selves...celebrated itself...themselves. And I knew now that this long hike was merely one more opening up, one more brilliant spotlight illuminating that glorious rainbow-hued, spectral fan of the tail—my peacock's tail—all our peacocks' tails that continue opening and revealing themselves...forever.

You and I are unit parts of the one great all-embracing Nature. (If you prefer to use the word God, Creation, Infinite, *who shall disagree?) The broad aim of nature is evolution— constant growth to higher levels of perfection ...expressed by the highest attributes which we know inwardly should be strived for.*
—MARK GILBERT

REFLECTIONS

The Stream

It was a rather small stream as streams go but it was very pretty —sun-dappled, cool to my bare feet floating in its softness, rippled with the fresh-burst colors of early Spring, and chittering in whispery mantras over the rocks and through the shallow, shadowed places.

At first my mind wandered lazily, randomly, as it tends to do when I'm in secret, silent spots like this. But then the thoughts came, one by one, like little drops of dew trickling through my head and settling into small still pools on the pages of my journal:

> I'm looking at the veins in this bright new leaf and then I'm looking at the veins on the back of my own hand (admittedly a little gnarled and worn) and seeing how interrelated everything and everyone on our little planet is, and knowing how obvious it all is if we just stop for a moment and see.

*Loving one thing or one person totally
without all those petty reservations
is to love everything
and everyone.*

✐

*Voices, voices, voices—all chattering away
        happily together in my head
And—God bless 'em—they're all mine!*

✐

*The chains that bind
that endure over time
are the chains of life
unbroken by all the terrors and all the strife
and bound together by the might
of love.*

✐

*All the answers are already here, and always
        have been,
it's just the questions we keep forgetting.*

✐

*The longest journey of all—
that sparkling, zany, terrible, wonderful,
        frightening, fantastic
infinite journey—
is the journey*

within...
deeper and deeper and deeper.

Go ahead—lose your-self, cast it to the wild
        winds
of adventure and serendipity
and watch in wonder
as all your other selves
emerge
Smiling and thankful.

Isn't it amusing and silly
how sure we all pretend to look and be
in our absolute sureness
of nothing
at all.

Freedom is knowing your needs
and laughing
at how simple
they are.

We're only exploring and adventuring
back
to where we all began.
In infinite perfection.

This tree I'm stroking now
is a universe.
You've just got to see it
that way.

The more I learn,
the more I learn
to unlearn.

So many moments
in a single moment.
No one is ever
complete.

I hope all this
never
ends;
I hope
I never
arrive;
I hope
it is
always
now.

Almost Gone #3
Riptides and Riddles

Your selves really emerge when you are
slipping away.

"*Exmouth,*" the colorful brochures proclaim, "*Where it's sum-mer all year round!*"

From what I'd heard of the real Australian 120-degree summers here, this kind of hook seemed of questionable appeal, but the manager of the Exmouth Coral Coast Tourist Bureau insisted that constant sea breezes and low humidity made Ningaloo and Exmouth ideal future resort areas.

Future resorts!? I'll take it just the way it is now, thank you, with emus pecking at the scrub on the edge of town, kangaroos hopping between the water holes on the flats below the craggy clefts and canyons of Cape Range, and the utter peace and silence of the white arced beaches of the Ningaloo Coral Coast. Two ospreys floated high above me. Tiny white ghost crabs scattered like surf froth as I walked barefoot on the warm sand. Geckos darted between sprays of spinifex on the low dunes.

I enjoyed a couple of utterly indolent, do-nothing, dawdle days here and, as a final gesture to the region's most notable attraction—the great Ningaloo Reef—a Great Barrier Reef of the Australian west coast, I decided to join a handful of other travelers on a glass-bottom-boat excursion among the colorful corals.

For an hour or more we drifted in the shallows, watching the parrot fish, groupers, red emperors, eels, coral trout, starfish, sea slugs, and enormous turtles among the multicolored explosions of coral heads. After a while, though, seeing such sights through the thick glass of the boat was no longer enough and a number of us decided to go snorkeling. We wanted to float among the fish and lose ourselves for a while in the sun-dappled shadows of the coral forests.

I lost track of time.

Coming to the surface a while later I realized that all the others had gone back to the boat. I could see them perched on the bow in a group, drinking, and doubtless listening to the skipper telling tall tales of the reef. They all had their backs to me, rock music was playing and no one seemed in any hurry to return to shore.

Five more minutes, I promised myself, and disappeared again into the cool depths, playing with the fish and watching the shards of sunlight undulate over the exotic coral formations that faded into the deep purple shadows.

Then something rather odd began to happen. As I lay motionless close to the surface I noticed that the coral was drifting past me. Slowly at first, and then with increasing speed. A rather pleasant sensation—like peering through the window of a moving train. Only I sensed I was being pulled farther and farther away from the boat.

I came to the surface again. I *was* being carried away from the boat. I could see my fellow snorkelers still drinking and listening to the skipper's tales, but they were smaller now and the boat was a good quarter of a mile away.

No problem. Time to swim back and join the fun.

Only the swimming didn't seem to work. I increased my pace, but the boat came no closer. Something was carrying me farther out into the ocean. The water was noticeably colder too. And waves were forming in a breeze that had not been there before. Small waves at first, hardly chin height. And then a little bigger.

O.K.—power-swimming time. I switched to a steady crawl, but the boat remained just as far away. And the wind became stronger, blowing directly against me. Only one thing to do. Bawl out and tell the skipper to come closer.

I took off my mask and shouted, but my voice didn't seem to carry. I shouted louder, but now the wind was blowing the sound back into my face. I tried waving, but no one was looking in my direction. They didn't seem to know I was out there. Maybe they assumed I was already somewhere on the boat.

I opened my mouth for a real bellow, and a wave—a wave I should have seen but didn't—crashed into my face and sent water tumbling down my throat and windpipe.

I was gagging. I swung around away from the boat, letting the waves pound the back of my head. If I could just get my breath back and my mask on...the mask! Where the hell was my mask? Dammit, it must have been knocked out of my hand when that first wave hit. Now I could hardly breathe in those waves that thrashed between me and the ever-receding boat.

For only the second time in my life (the first was when I was seven, and I'd almost forgotten it) I became scared in water. Initially it was just a little frisson of fear, a faint shiver up the spine. Water has always been my friend, something to frolic in, something to love for its buoyancy, its colors, its dappled intricacies. But now it became an attacker. An enemy. My breath was still weak as the windpipe struggled to clear itself.

Panic hit. I couldn't reach the boat, I couldn't make them see me, and I couldn't make it to the shore that was well over three miles away. My energy was draining as I dog-paddled with my back to the waves.

Turn around again—keep your mouth shut—and wave like crazy!

The waves hit hard again, angry now. White-topped and cold. I turned and waved as vigorously as I could with both arms, pushing my body out of the water.

Dammit, couldn't anyone see me? Bloody idiots! Didn't they know I was here? I wasn't going to be able to do this many more times.

I felt the adrenaline surge but knew that my strength was running out fast. My heart was pounding. My arms felt leaden. My breathing was hoarse, fast, and shallow. Panic grew as I realized the horrible inevitability of what was happening; it seemed to tighten my lungs so that I had almost no air.

Strange things were going on in my brain. Two entirely different reactions. One-half seemed to be a miasma of panic and pain from a body too tired now even to swim. The other half was a brilliant kaleidoscope of moving images, a series of fast-forwarding tapes, replaying fragments of memories, sensations, emotions. Friends' faces flashed by. A sudden picture of me crying as a child when I'd accidentally tipped my baby sister out of her carriage. A fight I'd once had with a bully in school back in Yorkshire. My father's rare but always loving grin. My first car, a bright turquoise-blue Austin Mini, and the pride of that first drive. A lobster feast on Cape Cod with friends from New Jersey. Our first New York apartment with a tiny terrace on the fringe of Greenwich Village. A sudden taste of blinding-hot Indian vindaloo curry and then Anne, smiling, laughing, and a thought—*Oh God! She's going to be really pissed if I don't get home*—a crazy vivid patchwork of unpatterned images.

And then from a newly emerging third part of my brain—something, somewhere, cool and objective—came a quiet, almost disinterested voice telling me, *You're drowning, David. You'll be done with all this soon and you'll be all right. There are many more things to come—things you never dreamed of...*

I could see, not feel, but really *see* myself dog-paddling more slowly now as if I were an impartial voyeur in my own demise. The energy was fading, the cold being replaced by a strange warm glow. I'd never had an out-of-body experience before, but that's how it felt—as though part of me, the essential part, was above the thrashing waves, maybe twenty, thirty feet above, looking down at the pathetic little flailing figure below, waving its arms, fighting the inevitable.

And there were more things to come. A calm. An acceptance. A sense that for one of the few times in my life I was utterly helpless, that there was nothing "I" could do, and that me, my fate, my life, all the me-s that are me, were being given over to something else, something much larger, all-encompassing, something that would take care of me.

I didn't really sense the arm encircle my neck at first. It felt, I suppose, like another wave, another battering. And then, with a jolt, my three free-wheeling brains melded back into a single entity screaming out one very clear message: You're being choked!

The arm was like a vise, compacting my windpipe and squeezing out the last gasps of air. I lashed out, but the arm tightened even more. Maybe fearing that my apparent panic would destroy us both, my rescuer was determined to control my movements. I managed to turn enough so that he could see my face—now in the final stages of asphyxiation!

"Shoulders! I hold your shoulders..." Somehow the words spluttered out.

Whoever my savior was, he nodded, turned, and I swam weakly with him against the waves, one arm across his back, gripping his shoulder. I still had little air in my lungs, but I knew now I was safe, and there was no panic. Just a determination to get back to the boat without making an utter fool of myself.

Faces peered over the bow, arms reached out, and I was dragged slowly on board. Someone thrust a glass of something sweet and strong into my hand. It burned like ice and fire, but it did its work, making me choke out the seawater in my lungs and sense the warming fingers of sugary alcohol ease through my body.

I was utterly drained. There was no energy left. The boat bobbed about in the heaving swell. Then I heard the motors roar and watched us drawing closer and closer to hard land, safe, dependable land.

I just wanted to be laid out on warm sand well away from that pernicious ocean and left to sleep and sleep.

A great traveler...is a kind of introspective; as he covers the ground outwardly, so he advances fresh interpretations of himself inwardly.
—LAWRENCE DURRELL

REFLECTIONS

Releasing My Inner Woodsman

It was an ancient and lopsided shack and I found it by chance on a back road that dead-ended nine miles deep into the vast Baxter Forest wilderness of northern Maine.

Someone way down in the valley told me it was at least one hundred years old and built by fur-trappers when fur-trapping was big business in these remote parts. Someone else advised me to keep away: "S'not empty," he warned. I assumed he meant someone was occupying it. "No," he said with a strange laugh, "but somebody's sure there."

I don't believe in ghosts. Well, not much. And I wanted the experience of living alone in the woods for a while. So I ignored the warnings, bought a load of supplies, drove back deep into the forest, and moved in.

The first couple of days were just fine. Peace, solitude, absolute silence except for the wildlife, which was pretty benign. No bears, no wolves (a shame really—I'd have liked a few tall tales to tell on the road). But the guy in the valley was right. There were *people in that cabin. I never saw them but they certainly saw me and they moved into me as easily as I'd moved into their home. I felt as if I were being led deep within, tapping knowledge and understanding previously unrecognized and certainly unused. Whenever I was*

about to do something foolhardy or, in some instances, downright dumb, I'd feel a nudging or a gentle restraint and a sense of being guided by an utterly invisible presence (no ghostly wraiths etc. whatsoever!). Although I've never had an elder brother or formalized "mentor" figure in my life, I imagine I would experience similar sensations of nurturing, caring, and unpatronizing support.

I stayed far longer than I'd intended and when I finally decided to move on I'd learned quite a lot about how to hunt with a homemade bow, how to split logs, how to tickle a trout in a stream for supper, how to identify the creatures around the cabin by the way the undergrowth crackled and crunched, when a storm was on its way, and where to find safe wood-food—mushrooms, berries, salad greens, the lot.

Before my arrival here, I'd known none of this. Nothing. Nada. But when I left I was a woodsman of sorts—taught not by "how-to" manuals and the like but by my friends who lived here, silently looking after me, introducing me to the ways of the woods, reviving long-dormant and ancient me-s in me—the ones who knew and loved and survived in wild places like this eons ago.

I want to be alive to all the life that is in me now, to know each moment to its uttermost.
—KAHLIL GIBRAN

An Aboriginal Dreamtime Odyssey

We are, all of us, created anew each day.

I was cold. Very cold. Despite the daytime furnace heat of Australia's outback, a numbing nighttime chill invariably settles across the vast shrub-dotted plains of the interior, sending most living things—myself included—into a somnolent stupor. The silence was tangible—a zenlike void—slowly filling with a delicious anticipation of dawn. The star-speckled blackness of the night sky gradually eased into a purple-gray half light and then slowly—ever so slowly—the sun rose in a great golden yolk of light and heat and Uluru (Ayers Rock) emerged, red and wraithlike, from the vast flatness. Colors spread in a slow tide across the desert. I was here—I was really here! After a long flight and a switch of planes in Alice Springs, I had arrived at last in the heart of Australia's Red Center, at its very navel, and was about to experience the daily rebirthing of the world's largest (1,142 feet high) sandstone monolith, set in the middle of more than 2 million square miles of flat Outback on the earth's most ancient landmass, eroded to a virtual peneplain over 3 billion years.

Years ago, Bruce Chatwin's unusual book *The Songlines* touched something deep within me. He was describing the Australian Aboriginal's "Dreamtime" creation stories in which an unformed world had been shaped by ancestral beings—a myriad of giant-sized kangaroos, lizards, birds, snakes, cater-pillars, witchetty grubs, even sea creatures, plants and cloud-beings—that emerged from the void and journeyed widely creating all living things and all the features of the landscape—water holes, mountain ranges, scarps, rivers, everything.

Uluru and the nearby Olgas cluster of thirty-six smooth-domed hills (now known jointly as the Uluru-Kata Tjuta National Park) remain today as physical evidence of the ances-tors' feats enacted in the creation, or Dreamtime, period. The Anangu—or Aboriginals—who today number around 250,000 throughout Australia, are the direct descendants of these beings and have the eternal responsibility of perpetuating and caring for the land through "singing" the ancient rituals of stories, songs, dances, and *corroboree* ceremonies along the Iwara, the dreaming tracks or "songlines" reflecting the ances-tors' journeys. The secrets of these tracks are passed on by complex initiations from generation to generation in the form of the Tjukurpa, or Aboriginal laws, that rigidly define the relationships between people, plants, animals, and all the phys-ical features of the land. Chatwin wrote of the ancient ances-tors, "They wrapped the whole world in a web of song," which I found a wonderfully evocative description of Creation, and he emphasized the heavy duty placed upon today's Aboriginal people to maintain the songlines through constant rituals, because "an unsung land is a dead land."

As I read deeper into Chatwin's book I knew that one day I would come to the Australian outback and learn more of its mysteries. And voila!—here I was—watching the sun turn Uluru into a towering crimson reality and walking with a few others around its five-and-a-half-mile base as a guide told us the intricate Dreamtime tales of its creation, showed us hidden water holes and led us under rock overhangs to peer at ochre-painted rock art created by Aboriginal ancestors over 20,000 (some experts claim over 50,000) years ago.

Despite all the charms of Uluru and its modern Yulara hotel complex, I found the place a little too crowded for my earth gypsy tastes and felt a need to pull away and seek out something less tied to time and schedules and tourist pick up/drop off points. Something that would allow me to explore the underlying realities of this region, those tantalizing flickers of perception that came to me when I looked into the eyes of Aboriginal guides and sensed timeless realms of knowledge so alien to our contemporary rush-rush, affluenza-plagued lifeways.

And things happened, as I knew they would. By chance I met a charming young woman who was in the process of developing small-group trips south from Yulara deep into the lands of the Pitjantjatjara people.

So—I set off the following day in a rented Land Cruiser with one of her guides, Lynne, on a long, bone-jarring drive south along red dust tracks. The scrub-dotted desert, flat and seemingly featureless, makes you constantly aware of the vast immensity of the sky. Below is an infinite rust-red nothingness, a place where distances are measured by the earth's curvature and diffused by shimmering heat hazes; above is that arching sky dome so pure-blue it makes your eyes ache. When the occasional cloud appears it is a singular event. I watched as a huge thunderhead evolved out of the nothing in the west and ballooned ominously into an imposing object thousands of feet high, which gave the sky even greater vertical dimension and seemed, by its very immensity, to compress the already flattened earth into even greater insignificance. How small, alone, and utterly frail seems man! To survive here, to find purpose and nourishment here, you *need* the company of Dreamtime creatures and the security of dreaming tracks or songlines for navigation, water holes, and bush food. You also need utter faith in your oneness with everything around you, bound unerringly by Tjukurpa law, laid down and maintained in perpetuity, celebrated, sung, and resung to provide finite edges and realities in this otherwise unreal, edgeless infinity. Even if there wasn't a God, a greater creative mind, you'd certainly have to invent one and learn to understand his ways, otherwise your ability to survive here and find daily nourishment would be destroyed and your rapid extinction guaranteed.

The next few days presented me with an experience I'll never forget. With Lynne as my guide and interpreter I lived

bush-style in a small campground set against high red cliffs at the edge of a vast mulga bush plain studded with thousands of red-mud termite mounds. At night I slept under dazzling stars in the traditional bushman's swag (a hefty roll complete with pillow, mattress, and sleeping bag all wrapped in sturdy waterproof canvas) and during the days spent most of my time in the company of two elderly Pitjantjatjara women, Nganyinytja and Tjulkiwa, their husbands, Ilyatjari and Mutju, and members of their extended families. Nganyinytja was the spokesperson and explained how she welcomed visitors to her remote homeland: "I want to teach all people, black and Gadia—whitefellas—about the land and our way of living with it. If people will listen to our way then they will understand why we Anangu still live in this country—our country— and keep the old ways, the Tjukurpa laws, and sing the spirit of our land. We want to increase understanding and acceptance of each other. The wind that blows across our country talks to everyone and they begin to realize that we all share the same spirit. We are all of one same earth."

Nganyinytja spoke softly and gently. "I do not talk badly of those people who do not understand," she told me, even though the terrible stories of her husband, Ilyatjari, about the mistreatment of Aboriginals by early white settlers and pastoralists made me squirm with outrage. "There is a revival—people will come here from all over the earth and see how we live and they will learn that it is good—they will learn to care for the land again; they will take something valuable back with them."

My initiation into the "old ways" came slowly, but it did come. The apparent void of the land began to give of its secrets. I learned where to find witchetty grubs (deliciously crisp peanut-flavored snacks when roasted—honestly!) under the ground among the witchetty bush roots; I began to spot bush-tucker in the sparse desert fruits—small bush plums, tomatoes,

peaches, and figs; occasionally I thought I could tell the difference between old and new trails left by rabbits, kangaroos,
lizards, and snakes, and distinguish the liquid presunrise calls
of the black-and-white pied butcherbird and the chiming
wedgebill from the rich dawn chorus of mulga parrots, cocka-
toos, willie wagtails, bowerbirds, and cooing crested pigeons.
I even learned the crafty ways of honey ants whose false trails
and chambers eventually led to a deep subterranean cavern of
delights where they hung in hundreds, their abdomens bloated
like little grapes, ready to be sucked clean of their delicious life-
giving nectar.

Family members showed me how to use simple but effec-
tive hunter-gatherer implements—the digging stick, the spear
and spear-thrower, the boomerang, the *piti* and *wira* dishes
carved from mulga tree bark, and the grinding stones for making breadcakes from grass seeds. They explained how ancient
Dreamtime laws create a cohesive framework for mutual support and order; they told me how the constant singing and
walking of traditional Dreamtime tracks (each initiated member of the family "mob" has his or her specific totemic ancestor
who defines tracks and sacred places to safeguard) combined
spiritual duty with pragmatic land maintenance through scrub
burning and water-hole cleansing. I learned of their bush medicines, the importance of secret male and female "business" rituals, the crucial initiation of young family members to
perpetuate the Tjukurpa laws, and their delight in ancient
dances and in creating elaborate sand paintings. These exquisite
dot-filled Dreamtime artworks are now produced on bark and
canvas by scores of Aboriginal artists in Outback communities
and can be found in galleries and stores throughout Australia.

Despite all my experiences and learnings, I seemed to be
floating on the edge of Aboriginal Dreamtime, sensing elusive
mysteries. At first my pragmatic Western mind dismissed the

idea of supernatural powers possessed by Aboriginals as merely the ramblings of overactive minds entranced by the enticements of half-understood myths and superstitions. But the families' openness and unhyped honesty began to make me wonder about such abilities as bodily transcendence of enormous pain and near starvation, the life-and-death power of "bone-pointing" rituals, the transmutation of form (from human to animal and vice versa), the possibilities of rapid healing using ageless bush remedies, the existence of widespread mental telepathy between clan members, the ability to "go invisible" or appear in multiple form, even claims of levitation and instant bodily transference from one place to another.

My slow acceptance of these possibilities came, not in any hocus-pocus, drug-induced or magical sleight-of-mind manner, but only after listening to the families and observing their quiet certainty, their matter-of-fact acceptance of such actualities as a natural outcome of their ability to instinctively tap deeper energies and powers—powers that our contemporary world has long since forgotten or replaced with more tangible, material, and pragmatic realities.

I remember one small incident in particular. At night when the families decided it was time to sleep they moved away from the campfire to different locations in the mulga scrub. Following the first coloring of dawn, when the birds began their liquid chatterings, they would ease up out of their swags and sit in silence for a long time. I could see all the families doing the same thing—just sitting in silence, no one moving.

After maybe twenty minutes of the strange stillness, Mutju rose to stoke up the fire. I followed him.

"Why all that long silence?" I asked him. He smiled—a little benevolently—on this uninitiated outsider.

"We were talking," he said.

"I didn't hear any talking."

He sighed—a how-dumb-can-you-be kind of sigh. "Not word-talking. That kind of talking is not necessary. We know each other. We hear each other. We understand each other."

He could see I was still a little perplexed. "I am me," he explained slowly, "but I am also each one of them. They are they but they are also me. We hear one another quite clearly because we are all part of the same thing—the same person. The silence you heard was full of conversation." Then he laughed. "Help me with the fire. You're hungry." And he was right. I was very hungry. Hungry for knowledge. I sensed worlds of wisdom wormed away in this fading and amazingly ancient culture.

✍

Another incident occurred a few days later. My "hunger" was slowly being replaced by a gradual acceptance of things I could not easily explain, and this particular event helped spur my esteem for the unexplainable. It was in the evening before dinner. We were all sitting around the communal fire in a clearing edged by mulga scrub. The searing heat of the day had been replaced by a soft warm breeze that rustled the leaves like ghostly whispers. The food—an enormous kangaroo tail this time (and unlike the taste of so many exotic meats, this in no way resembles chicken)—was being prepared by two younger women, and the elders had ceased their incessant prowling for kindling and dry branches for the fire. There was little talking. We just sat in the purpling twilight watching the flames and laughing at the children chasing one another around the man-sized termite towers that rose in their thousands across the plain.

Then a cry came—a sudden shriek of surprise and pain. One of the children had fallen over a rock. The other children were giggling and cheering at first but then their voices went strangely silent. We all stood up and walked across to the fallen figure. It was Abaco, one of Nganyinytja's grandchildren, a boy of four or five with huge eyes and an enticing lopsided grin. But there was no grin now and his eyes were squeezed shut in pain. He made soft whimpering sounds and held both hands over his right leg. One of the men eased them away and the sight brought an abrupt weakness to my knees. Abaco's leg was completely broken, with a small part of the bone showing through his soft, bronze skin. I had never seen such a vicious break although thankfully it appeared to be a single fracture. Gently I was pushed away. The women, without any hesitation, went off into the bush looking, I was told later, for poultice leaves and other bush medicines. The men gathered around the boy in a tight circle and Mutju, who seemed to be regarded as the family leader in times of crisis, asked them to hold Abaco, whose eyes were now open and streaming with tears. Mutju stroked Abaco's forehead and leaned close to his left ear, whispering something to him over and over again. Abaco seemed to relax. His whole body eased on the dusty earth and his eyes closed slowly, almost as if he was in some kind of hypnotic trance.

Mutju then placed each of his huge hands on either side of the broken bone and gently kneaded the soft flesh of Abaco's leg, feeling the extent and angle of the fracture. His kneading gradually became a long slow massage around the bone. The other men watched him with respect while continuing to hold Abaco's body firmly. Then—in a movement so fast it seemed never to have happened—Mutju pulled both ends of the leg apart in a sudden swift motion. The broken bone disappeared beneath Abaco's skin, and there was a decisive click. One of the men handed Mutju a long torn strip of cloth, which he bound rapidly and tightly around the reconnected bone. Abaco still seemed to be sleeping. His body had jerked when the bone clicked back into place but he gave no sign of having felt any pain.

The circle gathered closer now around the little body. Each man placed his right hand on the boy's leg and utter silence settled over the huddled group. The sky was deep orange behind the mulgas, the breeze had ceased and a great stillness eased over the edgeless plain. No one moved. No one spoke. Abaco's leg was totally hidden by hands, which remained motionless until the women returned with leaves and whatever medicines they'd been gathering in the surrounding bush.

Throughout the long night and the next three days there were always two family members at Abaco's side, changing the leaves, resting their hands on his leg and feeding him medicinal liquids made from the gathered plants. At certain times eight or nine people would be hunched around him, always silent, always touching and caressing the leg. I had given up asking questions. I always received the same answer anyway—"We are in the healing."

On the fourth day Abaco was sitting up, eating voraciously like an adult, smiling and singing with Tjulkiwa. On the fifth day he was walking again with only a small binding of leaves on his leg. No limp, no pain, no apparent distress from his ordeal. "He is healed," said Mutju without any trace of complacency. I watched Abaco kick his ball, a little gently at first, and then with almost all of his old vigor. He appeared to be healed alright!

⌀

On my last evening Nganyinytja suddenly announced it was "time for dancing" and supervised the elaborate body dot-painting of herself, Tjulkiwa and young children of the family. She used her own white dyes and twigs whose ends had been pounded to fibrous paintbrushes to create ornate whorls and spirals of dots on their chests, shoulders, and arms. Within the patterns were ancient symbols of Dreamtime creatures reflecting the different songs that each member of the group is obliged to "sing" throughout their lives to keep the land and the law intact for future generations. The children were silent and serious as their bodies were slowly and meticulously painted. Nganyinytja smiled at their stern little faces. "They know this is not a game," she told me quietly. "They will do the same with their own children one day."

Then she and Tjulkiwa stood and, humming rhythmic, dronelike songs together, led long shuffling dances with the children as dust rose from the dry earth and turned the sunset into a mystical golden-tinged haze. They continued for a long time as dusk crept across the mulga. The monotone sounds of their voices and their stately movements were mesmerizing and for a while I felt to be living in prehistoric times watching dances that had been danced by family ancestors for tens of thousands of years. Willingly I became a passive participant, sinking deeper and deeper into the old ways, into the Dreamtime.

Much later, when the dancing had ceased and we were all sitting together roasting just-caught rabbits on the campfire, Nganyinytja leaned over and touched my arm gently. "You are a little part of us now," she murmured quietly. I nodded and held her hand. My eyes were watering and it wasn't just from the campfire smoke.

Never forget—everythin's a mystery.
Once it stops bein' a mystery it stops bein' true.
—DAVID MOWALJARLAI, ABORIGINAL ELDER,
(QUOTED BY HARVEY ARDEN IN *DREAMKEEPERS*)

I Am Home

In this far, far place
—I am home.
In this simple meal I share
red beans and rice on broken plates
with this old couple high in these lonely hills
—I am home.
In the heart of this father
singing softly
to his baby, barely born
—I am home.
In the wild, questing eyes
of this young boy
riding his slow tired pony
and thinking him a speed-stallion
—I am home.
In the tribesmens' whirling dance
by the crackling, sparkle-light
of a bush-scrub fire
—I am home.
In moments of open-eyed wonder when
the world is a big blue ball
of utter bounteousness
—I am home.
In everything and everyone that has
ever touched me
—and I, them—
—I am always home.

The Mysterious and Magical Lives of KC

The merest welcome into someone else's life can unlock the possibilities in our own.

Maine's lovely, lonely, pine-clad islands attract many offbeat characters. Some are the flotsam and jetsam of war traumas or of a world gone slightly wacko. They wash up on the shores at random intervals. Most stay only a short while, make a few bucks or live off scraps of welfare, and then move on in search of other places, other answers. A few stay and reinvent their lives and become, eventually, accepted "comers-in."

But then there are the "loners," the "hermits," the "gurus," who quickly vanish into the thick pine forests of these small, wild places, set up reclusive homes of sorts and appear only

148

once in a while to buy supplies before burrowing back again into the dark, silent interiors of these islands.

Totally by chance I found one such "hermit home" on a hike I took across the southern tip of a lovely island. I strolled through the thick, resin-scented forests and along the edges of small coves carved from the pink granite bedrock which gleamed and twinkled, its surf-scoured forms polished into shapes resembling soft, downy pillows.

The house was one of those places hopeful hermits dream about—a tiny, obviously self-built A-frame sheltered by pines and placed on a rocky ledge on the curve of a small cove with windows overlooking the ocean and a boat ramp of natural rock linking it to the tiny beach.

The yard was neatly organized: three piles of cleanly chopped wood—kindling to the left, fast-burning in the center and slow, all-night logs to the right; a stack of lobster traps surrounded by neatly coiled ropes, buoys, and a large blue plastic barrel for the catch; a generator and an outside refrigerator stocked with cold beer and basics; a small outbuilding used as a toilet. Everywhere a sense of perfect harmony and order.

I knocked on the door. There was no reply but a note pinned to the wall was one of the most welcoming I've ever seen:

> *Welcome—come on in—*
> *there's no dog to bite*
> *only water, food, and beer*
> *to keep you here*
> *til I return*
> *before the night. KC*

So—I let myself in and entered KC's little world.

The inside was similar to the outside, neatly organized, and consisted of a single room, around 20'x20', equipped with all the basics of KC's life—wood-burning stove and oven, battery-powered stereo and CB radio, sofa covered in an old quilt, scattered rugs, a well-stocked library with a distinct bias toward ecology, hand-built homes, carpentry, and small-scale farming. On the low table by the sofa was a manual for constructing a solar greenhouse, and in the corner by the stereo, a meticulous balsa-wood model of the house itself, obviously a feature of pride. What was not present was a TV, family photographs (at least not on display), dishwasher, microwave, washer-dryer, freezer, huge racks of pots and pans and dishes and dinner sets, bread-maker, pasta-maker, toaster, or any of that other stuff we seem to clutter our homes with.

Around the cooking/washing area was a raised platform reached by a rough-cut ladder, which contained a mattress covered by another colorful old quilt, a lamp, and more shelves of books. Sunlight trickled through segments of stained glass into the room, illuminating the floor and walls.

And that basically was it. A totally self-sufficient home—economical, extremely cozy, and full of the owner's—KC's—presence.

Or rather—presences.

For it was then, after I'd taken this initial inventory (in preparation for a spate of hermiting myself?) that the richness and variety of KC's lives—the remarkable range of interests and talents—began to open up in front of me. For a start I'd underestimated the scope of the library. Now I spotted organized groupings of books on nonfiction writing, screenplay writing, movie-making, interior design, gardening (yes, I later found an equally well-organized garden-in-miniature behind the house brimming with herbs, tomatoes, beans, and squash), hunting, boat maintenance, lobstering, gourmet cooking (primarily vegetarian), philosophy, invention-patenting, art (more than twenty manuals on watercolor and oil techniques alone), sculpture, herbal medicines, poetry, and a host of self-improve-ment and mystic works. And then there were some real oddi-ties on hologram design and manufacturing, hot-air-balloon designs, logo-creation and, strangest of all, an untitled book containing reproductions of ornate mirrors from countries all over the world, with, in each case, a silver mirrored surface which gave back faint reflections of the reader.

Then I looked at the walls. They were packed with oil can-vases and framed watercolors—mainly island landscapes and all bursting with the energy and confidence of an artist who understands his subject and knows what he wants to say and how to say it. And on every flat surface were sculptures—swirling, life-filled abstract forms in granite, wood, clay, and even a couple carved out of blocks of polystyrene—all signed KC. And on a long shelf below the stained glass window was a series of black files—some crammed with KC's poems, a non-fiction book on island living, a novel, two screenplays, a cook-book-in-progress with the working title *Nature's Bounty,* and a score of other KC projects.

I sat on the floor, exhausted and exhilarated. I felt I had walked directly into a stranger's head and been treated to a whirlwind guided tour of dozens of selves all gloriously ram-paging and roiling around this tiny A-frame shack on a little-known islet in Maine, two miles from the nearest paved road (actually the island had only one paved road) and a million miles from what passes as normal life in the world beyond this tiny cove.

I wanted to meet him (or her). And yet in a way, I didn't. It was enough to feel the energy, the presence, the range of tal-ents, the incredible array of selves so generously displayed and accessible to anyone who happened to be lucky enough to come across this hidden nirvana.

A little handwritten note tacked above the stove read:

*Ideas are as abundant as the stars in the universe...reach deep
into your own universe and take them. Your creativity will
bounce on the breath of the Creator's laughter and joy. KC.*

I waited for an hour and then decided to leave. But not
before scribbling a brief note:

> *To KC—whoever and wherever you are...*
> *I could easily have missed this place*
> *lost in the constant race*
> *of my own thoughts and mental din*
> *but I came, and have come on in*
> *as you suggest*
> *— and have been truly blessed.*
> *Thank You.*

And I walked back though the deep woods, singing and
tingling.

> *One of the most destructive forces is
> unused creative power. If a man out of laziness
> does not use his creative energy, his psychic
> energy turns to sheer poison.*
> —CARL JUNG

Tokyo—A Subway Named Desire

Exploring the needs of the carnal self is fun,
even if you don't indulge it.

I only came back for the noodles. Honestly. I really had no idea what I was about to experience in this sophisticated little Tokyo neighborhood, not far from that teeming city's touchstone of contemporary retail excess, the Ginza.

I was staying at a most unusual modern hotel, the Sofitel Tokyo, overlooking the vast forested lake and museum-dotted expanses of Ueno Park. I'd seen a photo of this towering oddity in a brochure and was fascinated by its Lego-gone-mad architectural extravagance—a soaring pile of irregular square blocks, each block containing four floors—some projected out, some recessed, and the whole thing looking as if a swift kick in a salient place would send it tumbling like a child's play-pile into the streets far below. (Inside, disappointingly, it's pretty much like any other high-rise hotel.)

Anyway. After photographing this architectural anomaly from every angle I decided to take a leisurely stroll to the Ginza and explore the legendary and exotic food courts in the basements of the great department stores lined up, one after another, in a welter of Japanese consumption-abundance.

The main streets were a little dull so I took a shortcut down an alley lined with tiny noodle shops where for $5 you could enjoy a generous bowl of slurpy wormlike udon noodles (slurping is not only inevitable, but obligatory etiquette in Japan) with scatterings of vegetables and chicken slices, all topped with a raw egg yolk. After the tenth shop, windows all crammed with brilliant color photos of noodle options and prices (or more elaborate, unbelievably lifelike plastic replicas of each dish), I gave in to a rumbling stomach, plonked down at a counter, and slurped away happily at my brimming bowl along with all the other seemingly always-hungry, always-nibbling, Japanese customers.

Refreshed, I continued on to the Ginza and spent the rest of the day gasping at the outrageous prices of clothing and ogling such oddities as a talking toilet seat, rice cookers, video-aquariums (a wide-screen high-definition TV set in a fish tank with bubbles, and a video loop of a huge carp endlessly swimming back and forth) and other electronic gizmos—most of the latter selling for twice the price of the same Japanese-produced items in the USA. The only time I sensed a real bargain was at the food court where, despite the ultra-inflated costs of items like chicken breast ($15/lb.), prawns ($30/lb.) and melons ($70 each!—but beautifully packaged), I managed to indulge myself on free samples of everything from sea urchin roe, smoked eel, shark ceviche and salmon caviar to teriyaki beef, tempura squash slices, and mini-wontons filled with lobster mousse. Most satisfying. I felt I had learned the secret to the thrifty life in the least thrifty of all world cities. Don't buy, just look, gasp in horror at the cost of everything and then fill up on the freebies.

By seven it was dusk and I set off walking, stuffed and satiated, back to the hotel. I chose another random alley-route but somehow ended up in the same noodle strip where I'd lunched. Except it wasn't the same place at all. The noodle shops were now mostly closed and the place had transformed itself into a frenetic nighttime neon fantasy world of karaoke rooms (the voices of a score of raucous rock star wanna-bes filled the street), hostess bars ($30 a drink with a guaranteed female companion to refill your glass at every opportunity and whisper sweet whatevers in your ear and then dump you at toss-out time), and "love hotels" (complete with photos of each available room—imagine the ultimate in "rococo-eroticism" featuring Pocono-style heart-shaped hot tubs and beds and then quadruple the garish glitter and flash). But most unexpectedly of all were the sex *Soaplando* establishments (apparently echoes of far earlier and less sophisticated antics in the public bathhouses), "total-strip" joints, and *pinku saron* (sort of "all you can eat and grope" establishments for the budget conscious), from which emerged the most amazingly beautiful and lithe female creatures in ultra-micros and navel-revealing tops barely the size of bras.

Japanese businessmen (Armani suits, Rolex wristwatches, alligator leather briefcases) strolled, or in some cases, caroused drunkenly, up the street and one by one disappeared under flash-and-flicker neon awnings to nefarious basement delights.

Well, I thought, I guess a noodle supper is out of the question here. And for that matter, so were all the *Soaplando* water-trade options. Not a single one of those gorgeous girls even gave me so much as a smile. A scattering of other gaijin (foreigners) were also receiving the same "don't exist" treatment. "They think we're too big," said one of them to me, gesturing suggestively with his hips. "And too dirty—they think we're diseased or something—and too cheap—costs $100 for twenty minutes in these places. Hell, back home in Texas I can git an hour for a coupla dime notes."

I was intrigued by the elegant "menus" of delights. No—not noodle menus but precise menus of exotic-erotic offerings outside each establishment with time limits and prices spelled out in elegant Japanese characters and Roman numerals. Naturally I couldn't understand any of the descriptions but I did notice there seemed to be an awful lot of zeros in the prices.

"Ah, very difficult," said a well-dressed Japanese gentleman whose level of inebriation did not entirely prejudice rational, coherent conversation. "If I translate it very embarrass, maybe."

"Oh no," I said. "I'm just curious. Just looking. No try."

"O.K.—so this one say, 'sponge bath with toys and two love girls...'"

Suffice to say that it would be inappropriate to continue this part of our dialogue any further. However, let us just note that whatever your wildest fantasies may be, I guarantee they pale into insignificance against the range of indulgences offered in this narrow alley, one of numerous similar alleys throughout Tokyo. All the options are there in glorious—if somewhat oddly nonerotic and antiseptic—array. And this in a country where imported pornography (even *Playboy*-genre magazines) and the more traditional slam-bang forms of prostitution are both officially illegal, and locally produced hard-core videos are "strategically blurred" throughout. In a country too where female modesty and formal dress codes are still the norm and overt public expressions of affection (even innocent hugs and

cheek-kisses in the street) are still considered vulgar and deca-
dently "Western."

My polite informant turned a little philosophical when I
expressed surprise at so many well-dressed *salarimen,* many of
them obviously on their way home to wives, children, and
houses deep in the endlessly sprawling suburbs of Tokyo, taking time out from their commute for a little "noodling" in noodle shop alley.

"Ah—very difficult explain. Shinto and Buddhism. Two
big Japanese religions. All mix up. Say we have two souls—
earth and top...high, you understand?"

"I think so. We have a similar idea in Western religion but
we're taught to feel guilt at the needs of the earth soul and
focus on the high—the heavenly one."

"Ah—ha, ha, ha!" (I love Japanese laughs. They always
sound so "written," each "ha" perfectly enunciated.) "Well—
that is problem for you. You go crazy! You needs please both
souls—low and up. Yin-yang. Otherwise..." He tried to sug-
gest, with an enthusiastic burst of spittle, the sound of a head
exploding. I nodded and admitted to myself that the potential
elimination of all the angst and pent-up frustrations created by
rejecting our earthy, lusty, sensual desires may save an awful
lot of psychiatric fees despite the fact that it runs counter to all
our indoctrinations and could lead to considerable confusion
and conflict on the husband/wife "faithfulness" front.

"So what does this menu say?" I asked, pointing to a particularly vibrant extravaganza of a neon sign filled with flashing outlines of martini glasses and curvaceous female forms.

"Ah. Special place. Fantasyland. Very...fun."

"What's a Fantasyland?"

"Ah well—there are three very popular fantasies about...
girls...that men have in Japan. Teacher with schoolgirl, man
patient with hospital nurse and *salariman* in subway car."

I nodded again. A quick peep at those amazingly ubiquitous and over-the-top hand-illustrated pornographic comic magazines in Japan confirms that these three "fantasies" indeed occur again and again in their steamy pages.

"How does it work? What happens in the subway car?"

"Ah, very simple. You go in room made just like subway car with seats and straps and train sounds...everything. Then people come in—men and young women—all dressed up and you all pack in together and then—for twenty minutes—you..."

"What?"

"Well...uh...you do what you like to do in crowded subway car when lovely girls are all pressed up all around you."

"You mean..."

"Of course..."

"How very...odd."

"Ah...yes. But very good for Shinto soul. Make you good husband. Good father. You have no..."

"Frustration?" I suggested.

"Frus...what is?"

"No hang-ups, no guilts."

"Ah—no guilties, yes. Spirit of Zen...live now!"

"Seems like a no-lose situation—for the man at least."

"Ah yes. And this is very good. No?"

I left the question unanswered, thanked the man for his guidance through this strange little netherworld of Japanese nookie, and continued my stroll up noodle alley toward my hotel. And I was still ignored by everyone despite my rather brief but colorful initiation into the mysteries of *Soaplando.*

"When in Tokyo...?" suggested my newly emerging Shinto-self, another possible contender for the ever increasing pantheon of selves-dom.

"Thanks, but no thanks," responded my dependable—but not much fun—higher soul.

"Y'know," said my stomach, which didn't seem particularly interested in any kind of soul at all—merely the zen of immediate hunger, "I could really go for another one of those big bowls of noodles."

> *Man is born to live and not to prepare to live.*
> —BORIS PASTERNAK

PUB PEARLS

Experimenting

"This word *holistic*. What d'you think it means?"

"So far as I know it means something that is complete and whole in itself but, at the same time, part of some other much larger whole."

"So what are we then?"

"We? You mean us? Us human beings?"

"Yeah."

"Well, we're obviously whole in ourselves otherwise we wouldn't be around talking and living and drinking and what-not."

"But what about the other thing? The bigger whole?"

"Ah—I don't think we've quite got that sorted out yet."

"Well, d'you think God's got it sorted out?"

"God!? Well—maybe he's experimenting too y'know, playing with all his options—just like us."

"You mean, God doesn't *know*?!"

"Pass on that."

I Am Bananas

*There are times when the vulnerable self takes
over. You need to listen to the knowledge of
your body and learn to rely on others.*

Around eight o'clock in the morning I knew something had
gone decidedly wrong. My mouth was dry and then full of sali-
va, then dry again. My body was sweating like a bilge pump,
streams of it, and the day's heat hadn't really hit yet; my simple cabin was still cool.

I had to get the bathroom—fast. And then again. And
again. By midday I'd spent most of my time there, and so far as
I could tell, I had nothing more to expel. But still I sat. Waves
of nausea flowed over me, sending hot and cold ripples up and
down my spine. The mirror on the wall showed a deathly face
edged in a moldy-green sheen and eyes so tired and egg-like that
I began to wonder if survival was in the cards at all.

Hour after hour passed. Time twisted in cobra coils. My
brain wandered around its confines like an inebriated slug.

Crazy thoughts kept popping up in utter free association. I was definitely in the throes of some emerging fever. All energy had long since been dissipated.

I moved to the bed and twisted and turmoiled. Occasional shards of sound came from outside: the surf, gulls, someone passing my cabin. The sounds became a series of symphonic variations, sometimes so distorted that I couldn't recollect what the original sound had been as my brain became a freewheeling bagatelle. The voices of passing children reverberated like gongs—booming, peeling, cymbaling into switchbacking roller coasters of sound.

By evening I was far out of the realms of reality. The fading colors played kaleidoscope forms on the walls; shadows became ogreish and then stretched out into landscapes with giant cacti, stunted trees, and shattered mountain ranges.

A butterfly fluttering through my open window became a kite, then a jeweled bracelet freely floating, then a silhouetted hawk, and finally a sinister, shadowy presence lurking high in the upper corner of my room. I think a lizard came in for a while, or a dragon or just another dream.

I stopped trying to make sense of anything. There was no me left in me. I was no longer fighting back, no longer interpreting and filtering—just letting the tides of images and sounds and smells and colors roll over me in this place where time had long since lost any meaning and I was free of everything.

On the second day—it seemed like the second day anyway—I had a vision. Something so clearly outlined and tangible that I reached out a long sweaty arm to touch...a basket of ripe bananas. Bananas? Something in the recesses of my battered brain was sending a message. Bananas. I had to get some bananas!

Someone was passing the window. I could hear voices. But I couldn't get off the bed. I could hardly lift my head. So I reached out for something hard and found a book I'd been reading before my world collapsed. Gripping a corner as hard as I could I flung it at the window. The noise of the impact was wonderful, the first recognizable noise in almost two days. Swish, thunk, kerplop. Welcome, real-world sounds.

The voices stopped and I heard a slither of feet in sand. A face appeared at the window and a young boy peered into my shadowy room. Big black eyes, pink lips, bright teeth.

"Bananas, please. And Coca-Cola." It didn't sound like my voice. The boy didn't seem sure what to do. I repeated my request slowly and pointed to my mouth. A sudden smile and nod. "*Si*—bananas—*si, si*, Coca-Cola." And the face was gone.

More time passed, frozen shapes of time, each one distinct, glowing with different colors. An utterly new experience. And bananas were in there too. Curved scimitars, gleaming, voluptuous, linking loops of time like golden chains.

A knock. I said something but it came out a grunt. The door opened slowly. I thought I'd locked it, but it opened anyway and in came my little savior with an old battered tin bucket.

He stood by the bed and smiled.

Bananas.

He reached into the bucket and pulled out a stem of bananas —a dozen or more beautiful ripe fruits. And Coca-Cola. And papaya. There it was—sliced, wet, peach pink. The best papaya I had ever seen! I pointed to a pile of my usual traveling detritus on the dressing table—pens, notebooks, knife, film, and scrunched-up paper money.

"Take money," I thought I said, but it was another grunt.

"I come back—later," he said shyly and left with a smile, closing the door quietly behind him.

The next hour (I think it was an hour—time was still slithering around) was pure joy. Just the sight of the bottle and the fruit made me feel better. And never had Coke tasted so magnificent, that first fizzing gush, listening to it going down, filling all the oh-so-empty spaces in this useless lump of wet flesh I assumed was my body.

And the bananas! Such sweetness and softness. I could feel my digestive system eagerly sucking in every molecule of nutrition, every protein, mineral, vitamin, and whatever else that miracle fruit contains. If there's such a thing as fruit orgasm I had one as the sloppy pulp ran down my throat, my chin, my chest. In fact every sensory nuance of my body was besotted by the essence—the soul, the spirit—of bananas. Nothing else was getting in. Nothing else existed. My whole world, my whole being, every living, throbbing, pulsating part of me...celebrated in joy!

I slept a sleep of utter succulent peace. I think I dreamed I was a banana soufflé; certainly I felt all puffed up and mushy in the middle. Much, much later, deep into the evening, I awoke to find a plate of rice and more bananas, and another full bottle of Coke. The boy must have been back—all the old banana and papaya skins had been cleared away. A clean moist cloth covered my forehead.

I was safe. I'd come through the uninvited torment and turned up whole and alive on the other side, hog-happy in banana, Coke, and boiled-rice heaven. Who cares about yesterdays and tomorrows? I was here right now and being pampered like a prince in my modest palace, and the sunset was blasting through the window and those wonderful buzzing things outside in the trees were buzzing away again and doubtless more bananas were on their way.

I was very, very happy. How to describe it? Well, quite simply, I *was*...bananas!

> *You cannot travel the path until you have*
> *become the path.*
> —GUATAMA BUDDHA

Seeking the Hermit of El Tisure

A lot can be gleaned from those with certainty in their convictions.

It was one of those tales that makes the explorer in me come alive instantaneously.

"Somewhere, way behind these mountains," my inform- ant said, waving his hand to encompass the vast cloud-grip- ping Andean ridges that rose abruptly from the valley of this small Venezuelan town and vanished into an ethereal haze along the far horizon, "somewhere back there, but I'm not sure where, is a man who has become legend. He once lived not far away, down this valley, and was a wealthy man. And then one day he gave all his property to the town to be used to build a good school and clinic, and with his wife, a mule, some food and seeds and things, he went into the mountain to start a new life. And he's never been back here. Not once. His name is Juan Félix Sànchez and they say he is a hermit—a very strange hermit—and they say he has built his own church, all by himself, way deep in those mountains."

I was lucky. I found Paco, a young man who thought he knew where "The Hermit of El Tisure" (as they called him locally) lived, and he agreed to provide horses and be my guide. So, in a couple of days, we were ready and moving off.

The first part of the day was relatively easy going. Our horses cantered with graceful agility through the foothills cloaked in spiky *frailejon* grasses, but as the afternoon wore on the gradient abruptly changed from benign to boisterous and finally became a series of near-vertical precipices, which we climbed on foot along the narrowest of paths, tugging our now exceedingly reluctant horses behind us.

We barely had the energy to pull together a makeshift camp on a small rocky plateau before sleep overcame us. Sometime in the middle of the night I awoke briefly. It was very cold but there was no wind and no cloud. The black sky was a vast scattering of stars. The moon shone between the peaks of the mountains, silvering their summits. The silence buzzed in my ears. Only the soft breathing of Paco huddled in his sleeping bag reminded me where I was and what I was doing.

Dawn came as a fanfare, sudden surges of peach, and amber across the layered ranges. Far below, the tangled valleys were filled with lavender mists. Paco was already up, hunched over the butane stove trying to boil water for coffee (almost an impossibility at 12,000 feet). The animals looked fine, heads down, munching on the ice-flecked grasses. The sun rose rapidly; dun-colored peaks turned bronze and the whole mountain panorama beckoned us to move on, deeper into this "lost world" in the Venezuelan Andes.

We crossed over the second high pass and the descent was slow and difficult. Ice still coated the narrow path and we moved cautiously on the slippery rocks. But our spirits were different now. The worst had been overcome and we knew that somewhere down there, deep in one of the valleys, was a house, a shelter, a place to cook a decent meal—and Juan Félix Sànchez.

⌑

Finally, after two grueling days crossing the ranges, we saw the house—a rambling structure of black rock topped by sections of canvas and tin roof set against a hillside of wild bushes. There were no other buildings, no other signs of human habitation anywhere in that vast sweep of valleys and mountains. But curls of blue smoke, easing out from under the roof (no chimneys here), made the place seem friendly, beckoning.

As we approached we noticed small rock shrines, one in the shape of a cross, one a tiny chapel the size of a doll's house set by a swirling stream. We crossed the stream lower down and dismounted on a pasture of close-cropped grass at the side of the house. A cock crowed. A dog barked. Other than that there was no noise at all.

"This is the place. They will be inside," Paco said.

We crossed a second stream by way of a bridge of broad stone slabs and entered a dusty corral. Ahead of us a doorway led through to an enclosed courtyard. A couple of oddly shaped benches stood by the outer wall of the house, pieced together from wood planks supported by sections of twisted branches. On a low plank table lay two clay bas-reliefs. The clay was still moist. Someone had left them to dry in the sun. The figures were crudely shaped but it was obvious that they depicted scenes from the stations of the cross.

We entered a dark room built of black rock. Thin strands of sunlight filtered through chinks between the unmortared joints. Still nobody.

And then we saw the glow of a fire and a figure rose up, small and hunched. Another figure remained seated in the shadows. I groped forward across the earth floor. A hand—warm and rough-skinned—reached out. I saw a dark smiling face and a magnificent silver mustache. Eyes sparkled in the glow of the fire.

"I am Juan Félix Sànchez. You are welcome." He spoke Spanish in a slow gravelly voice. His hand gently squeezed mine and led me to a bench by the fire. "Sit down. You will have some tea."

At the mention of tea, the second figure rose.

"This is Epifania, my wife. She will make tea for you."

Whatever was in that odd-tasting brew quietly worked its magic. Within minutes I felt relaxed and refreshed. All the aches in my bones after that cold night on the mountain eased away.

It was time to get to know my hosts. The conversation was slow, punctuated by periods of friendly silence as we all sipped together. Juan answered all my queries quietly and politely as I tried to piece together the history of his unusual life. I asked why he had never returned to his hometown.

"There was no reason to go anywhere" he murmured softly. "Everything was here."

At one point, as he talked about his reason for the sudden change he had made in his life, he quoted something I couldn't quite understand. I asked him to repeat it and Paco translated:

The dead ones are not those who
rest in a cold tomb:
The dead ones are those who
have dead souls
and continue to live.

"Did you write that?" I asked.

Juan suddenly started chuckling and spilled tea over his stained trousers. "No, no. That is on the gate of a cemetery in Mérida. I remember reading it when I was a boy. But it is very true—yes?"

We laughed and nodded.

"A soul is all you have," he said. "Everything else is...you have to live....every minute of every day to the fullest and..." He shrugged again and left the sentence unfinished.

✍

In the late afternoon I was sitting with Juan on an old wooden bench set against the corral wall outside his home. We were both drinking more of that herb tea prepared by Epifania. She was a shy woman whose face was always partially hidden by the shawl draped over her head and held in place by a broad-brimmed straw hat.

The sun was still bright and hot, burning my face, as we laid our heads back against the wall and watched the chickens peck in the dust of the corral. On the hillside in front of us our horses nibbled happily on fresh green pasture. Behind them a waterfall tumbled off rock ledges into a series of cool, dark pools before becoming a stream again, chittering away behind us.

I turned to look at Juan. His eyes were closed now. His bushy, walruslike mustache hung down on either side of his mouth, which curved up slightly in a smile that never seemed to fade. His dark brown skin was lined and leathery, his chin fuzzy with a silver stubble of unshaved hair. For a man in his eighties he had the face of a mischievous boy—part cherub, part imp. His two pet parrots, bright green with red markings, cackled at one another while nibbling on a pile of sunflower seeds left by Epifania. There was a great peace about the place and I was glad to be here.

✒

Later on in the day I began to ask him about his church, built on a hillside a short walk from the house, but he seemed to grow impatient.

"Have you been there?" he asked.

"No, not yet. We've only just arrived."

"Well, go first. Then we talk."

Paco decided to stay behind and help Juan with some rock-lifting project (yet one more extension to the house?), so I walked over the pasture and across the stream alone.

The church came suddenly, round a bend in the track, perched on the edge of an alarming drop into the next valley. It sat, squat and compact, in bold stone simplicity on a sloping site, shaded by wind-shaped conifers. A twenty-foot-high stone tower with a belfry rose up beside the main door. In front was a tall cross decorated, Gaudi-like, in fragments of pebbles, pottery and glass. Small shrines and memorials to individuals known and admired by Juan filled the space between the church and the high stone retaining wall by the path.

I entered through a narrow gate and climbed the steps to the church. The blue painted iron door squeaked open. At first it seemed very dark, but as my eyes adapted to the glimmer of filtered sunlight, I found myself in a long narrow space about thirty feet long bound by more bare stone walls and with a sloping flagstone floor leading to an altar. A few chairs and benches made from more of those twisted branches and stumps so loved by Juan lined the walls. An enormous font, hollowed out by hand from a boulder, stood on a stone plinth decorated by chips of colored rock.

The power of the little church lay in its simplicity. It seemed to have grown directly out of the earth itself. For year after year, Juan and Epifania had built this place and its tower rock by rock and dedicated it to the Virgin of Coromoto. It's hard to imagine the energy, the sweat, the back-snapping toil that went into such an effort. And yet the church exuded a spirit of calm, peace, and effortlessness. In the same way that the great pyramids seem by their overwhelming purity of form, to deny the agony and the superhuman labor that went into their construction, so here the clarity of Juan's vision seemed to suppress all thoughts of personal struggle during its creation.

I sat on the cold flagstones at the base of the altar for a long time. I'm not a religious person in any formal sense but Juan's little church touched something inside me. Maybe it was the sureness—the certainty—of his own faith. Surrounded by all this evidence of his labor and his love, I felt a certain diffuseness, an uncenteredness, in my own ramblings and meanderings. While personally skeptical of rigid dogma and "only one answer" religious diatribes in all their many forms, I maybe am drawn a little too much into the "gentle anarchy" of my own life, avoiding spiritual commitment, sacrificing focus for the exploration of open-ended possibilities and alternatives. Most times I am content to play with the options, but once in a while, when faced with something as strong and moving as this place, I begin to wonder...

And there was more wonder to come.

I opened the door of the church and stepped out into—nothing! The earth had vanished. Everything was pure white light. No mountains, no valleys, no trees—nothing but light. I blinked. It was cloud. Brilliantly glowing white cloud filling the valley and blocking out everything.

I wandered up the hill behind the church, carefully following the narrow path. The cloud whirled around me, blown by a strong wind. Then figures began to emerge, dwarf-sized and hunched among the *frailejon* grasses—wooden figures, carved with great boldness out of the limbs and trunks of pine trees. Juan's "Calvary."

It was an overwhelmingly powerful creation. In the rough-hewn and twisted figures of Jesus and the two thieves you could sense the horrible agony of death, and the grief of the carved mourners on the rock-strewn ground below the crosses. Behind the figures, Juan and Epifania had formed a pile of broken boulders to emphasize the remoteness and isolation of their depiction of Golgotha.

Then something very odd began to happen. As I stared at the tortured faces and the hands of Jesus outstretched in agony, the mists began to clear and sunlight touched the crosses and piled boulders. Within a couple of minutes the hill was once again bathed in brilliant afternoon light; the carved wooden bodies turned from a dead gray to a rich resin bronze. The place no longer seemed threatening and full of misery. There was a sense of new life now, new vigor in the figures—a resurrection in sunlight!

The cynical, agnostic part of my brain rebelled at such thoughts. I could sense it chuckling at the naiveté of this oft-confused individual, moved almost to tears by a trick of fickle microclimate—the sudden presence of warmth and light in the midst of a chilly cloud-bound afternoon. All the tangled thoughts of my night under the stars came rolling back; I could feel my agnostic self desperately trying to reduce the impact of the moment to the insignificance of overemotiveness and a passing hysteria.

But as I left the hill and the little stone church, something left with me...and has remained with me ever since...a sense of moving closer to the Calvary in my own soul—that place of sorrows and suffering from which, eventually, forgiveness and love spring freely and forever.

For once the self in me that wants to celebrate faith, trust and belief overcame the far more familiar cynicism of my doubter-self.

Looking back, I wish I had stayed longer and learned more from the "Hermit of El Tisure," but as he said in one of his indirect, enigmatic responses to yet another of my questions— "You can only learn what you already know. When you know all that you have always known, the learning is done."

> *Thou art a second world in miniature, the sun and moon are within thee, and also the stars.*
> —ORIGEN

A Mushroom High

Sometimes what you don't know can introduce
you to deeply hidden sides of yourself.

I was scampering over the soft white sands of Ko Samui and playing tourist again. A few years back, this island, way out in the Gulf of Thailand fifty miles north of Surat Thani, on the east coast of southern Thailand, was an undiscovered, palm-growing paradise. But word travels fast among the earth gypsy fraternity, and soon tiny palm frond A-frames were being built (in a day or two) by starry-eyed dropouts seeking another Goa for their endless revelries and reveries. And for a while it truly was. Money was virtually unknown on the island; the locals were friendly, sharing people; coconuts (the best in Thailand), fruit, free-range marijuana, psychedelic mushrooms, and fish were all available in endless supply. What more could true earth gypsies ever want! But gradually—maybe inevitably—the developers arrived with their upscale A-frame colonies, followed by trendy beach bunga-lows offering nightly beach parties, and finally the five-star resorts with every imaginable comfort at daily rates that are today the equivalent of a month's wages for your average Thai.

I'd been advised to avoid Samui's notorious psilocybin mushrooms. They were officially illegal anyway, following the deaths of a couple of overindulgent tourists. The tales of their demise varied. Some said they were convinced they could fly and had leaped off the high cliffs on Samui's eastern coast; oth-ers claimed they'd tried to play Neptune among the coral reefs and never returned. Whatever. Sadly, they had died, and it was all blamed on the island's hallucinogenic mushrooms, so the police decided it was time for a crackdown.

"Try some omelet."

I'd met a bunch of freewheeling Italian travelers. Now, Italians seem to have that knack of finding places and people that everyone else seems to miss—hidden beaches; unmapped mountain paths; an old woman in a palm-frond shack who cooks the most exquisite Thai curries brimming with prawns and lobsters; the quietest out-of-the-way places to camp. Wherever I go I look out for Italians—kindred spirits in my nooks-and-crannies ramblings.

"Is very good omelet. Have piece."

I should have known something was not quite right. There was too much giggling.

"Not bad," I said. And it wasn't. A rich creamy texture, laced with black flecks of what I thought to be truffles.

"Oh yes. Truffles. Just like truffles," they all assured me.

I ate a few more slices. They were all sharing their dishes, Chinese style; it seemed the sociable thing to do. Everything tasted so good. A wonderful spread, served by two beautiful Thai girls in a lopsided beachfront house of palm and bamboo, miles from anywhere.

We all ate slowly. There was no rush.

The only problem was my chair. I kept looking down to see if the legs were straight. I felt I was slipping sideways. Maybe it was the heat. Or those fiery little chilies—they can really make your head spin.

And then I was sitting on the sand, on the frothy lip of the ocean, quite a distance away from the table. I had no idea how I got there. I had no recollection of leaving the feast. But it felt O.K. The sand was warm, enticingly warm. Sensual. My legs moved backward and forward, digging deep into its softness.

So soft. Like duck down. And I was bouncing up and down—ever so slowly—like a baby on a puffy cloud. I could hear soft laughter behind me. Or was it a waterfall? Or a breeze in the palms? No matter. It was a lovely, gentle sound, trickling over my head like warm water, tickling my ears.

Someone put a glass of coconut milk in my hand. There was a face—one of the coquettish Thai girls. Peach-colored skin, flecked with the soft pollen of enticing adolescence, tiny pearl eyes, and a beguilingly coy smile. Her small oval mouth was moving slowly; I couldn't take my eyes off her teeth. Such neat, white, tiny teeth, like a miniature keyboard. I could reach out and play them and make wonderful music. But my hand didn't seem to want to move. I watched my fingers ease through the pink-gold sand like wriggling worms.

The sky was a blue I'd never seen before, a brilliant silky turquoise with a texture of soft tofu. It looked—well—it looked edible. As if I could reach out and cut pieces from between the cotton-candy clouds. And the clouds were different too—moving backward, then forward—gracefully, as in a slow minuet, leaving little images behind like lace petticoats.

Thoughts tumbled and swirled. Cascades of twirling perceptions, each one a different color and shape. Wouldn't it be fun, I thought, to slice through them and look at their cross sections—all those thoughts, colors and forms, all intertwined, all changing.

And then I was in the water. Again, no recollection of moving. I only remember thinking how nice it would be to float in the sea. It undulated, with dolorous surfing sighs, like a big rubber waterbed. Inviting. Promising. Tiny silver and gold fish moved between my toes. I heard a voice saying "f-i-s-h" very slowly. Sort of a surfy sound. "Fishhhhhhhhhh." A beautiful sound. Perhaps the most beautiful sound in all the world.

I was on all fours now. Some kind of creature. Maybe a large lizard playing in the shallows, seeing finger-long fish dart in shoals, scores of them turning as one, all intuitively of one mind. Then my hands became flippers. A seal now? As each flipper entered the water the shoals of fishlings would move away in sinewy curves and then curl back to look more closely, then curl away again as I moved forward, my body swaying from side to side. I could feel the sun's heat on my back, like massaging fingers, moving up my spine and outward across my waist and shoulders and tickling the underside of my chest.

Round pink boulders at the water's edge became enormous scoops of ice cream, piled on top of one another. A huge sundae. Particles of quartz sparkled like sprinkled sugar. I splashed water on the rocks and they darkened to a deep red. Raspberry syrup! How lovely.

Then my giggling began. Just ripples at first; it all felt so soft—pillowy—to this sea-frolicking lizard or whatever I was supposed to be, faced with all this ice cream. Except that I was changing now, rising up out of the water. I felt as light as a breeze. Lifting effortlessly like a seagull. As I moved my head, I seemed to lift even higher looking down at my ice-cream rocks and the water and the beach from up high. And I felt no weight. Nothing at all. I stretched out my arms, tilted to one side, and floated sideways. I lifted my neck and looked at the sky and moved upward, toward the blue tofu. I looked down and my body slid down through the warm air like a seagull riding the thermals. I was utterly free. I was a bird—a great wonderful winged creature floating on the spirals. I have never known such sensations except in dreams. I could feel the giggling rising from my stomach up through my lungs and throat and right out the top of my head—waterfalls of laughter, bringing more laughter, like a child, lost in the moment, in the fun of floating and laughing and soaring and diving...and the earth had never looked so beautiful...I wanted to dive deep into its gentle green softness....

Much, much later I landed gently and found myself sitting on the sand again. The sky was a more normal blue now and the pink rocks were—pink rocks. Pretty things, but rocks nevertheless. Certainly not ice cream sprinkled with sugar and laced with raspberry syrup. Silly idea.

My companions were all around, sprawled on the beach, asleep. One of the Italians rolled over, opened an eye, and smiled.

"Good omelet, I think."

The omelet. Of course. Those trufflelike flecks had been Samui psilocybin mushrooms. Sometimes I worry about me. I don't always catch on fast enough. But that floating bit really had been very, very pleasant.

"Meet anyone?' asked one of the girls.

"Y'know," I said slowly (very slowly—I still didn't feel in full control of my mind or my mouth yet), "I did. I certainly did."

Most people have that fantasy of catching the train that whistles in the night.
—WILLIE NELSON

Almost Gone #4
Disappearing Into Whiteness

*The outer world can lead you to internal places
of peace and silence.*

I had made a long journey deep into India's Rajasthan and had
enjoyed many adventures with the Maharaja of Jodphur, in the
golden city of Jaisalmer, and among tribespeople living way
out in the oases of that vast western desert.

But there was one place in that region that kept on beckoning me and I knew I had to go there.

It is called the Rann of Kutch. Those who know it inti-
mately call it "The White" and that's a pretty accurate term for
what is a vast, flat salt desert, more than 400 miles long and
over 200 miles wide in some places, which for the most part

JAISALMER
— India

consists of nothing else but eye-searing swaths of gleaming white salt, flat as a floor and disappearing into infinities in every direction.

Why go? I often asked myself as my jeep churned and creaked across that blond gray desert following a very fickle trail of packed earth that kept disappearing in long patches of windblown sand resembling miniature dunescapes.

The only answer I could come up with (after Sir Edmund Hillary's "because it's there") was that after all the tales I'd heard from villagers about "The White," of friends and families lost forever over its trackless horizons, I wanted to experience what they described as "nothingness"—a featureless space of white on white on white.

So here I was, feeling a little trepidacious, but driven by a compelling curiosity. And now the mood of the desert had changed and there was not a tree or shrub or even a single

blade of grass anywhere. Nothing but an endless, blankness in every direction. The track had been reduced to a vague incision in the salt, but beyond that was what I'd come all this way to see. Nothing at all. Eighty thousand square miles of perfect white flatness. No movement. No life. Nothing.

It was like vanishing into some vast realm beyond the mind, way beyond thoughts, beyond feelings and sensations and all the convoluted tangles of consciousness. Even beyond awareness itself. A space so colorless, so silent, and so infinite that it seemed to be its own universe. And I just simply disappeared into it.

The sun was so hot in the dry air that I almost felt cold. I noticed this odd sensation at one point, about ten miles into the whiteness, when I got out of the jeep and walked across the cracked surface of the salt. After a couple hundred yards, however, I realized I had been a little careless. The heat shimmers were so violent that I could no longer see the vehicle. I couldn't even see my own footprints because of the hardness of the salt and the intense sheen radiating from it. Then I noticed my shivering, similar to the sensation of a burning fever when the hotter your body becomes, the colder you feel. It may also have been a flicker or two of fear. I realized the implications of my stupidity. Two hundred yards away from my landmark was the same as a hundred miles. I didn't know where the hell I was. I was lost in a miasma of brilliant, shimmering white light.

I remembered tales of arctic explorers caught in sudden blizzards and dying in frozen confusion a few blinding yards from their tents. A few yards in a blizzard is infinity. This too was infinity.

In retrospect the whole incident seems ridiculous, but at the time I sensed panic and the horrible reality that if I didn't retrace my steps within the next half hour or so I'd become a raving sun-sacrificed lunatic lost in this utter nothingness. Given shade I could have waited for the sun to drop and the shimmers to dwindle. But shade was as impossible as alchemist's gold here. There was no shade for over fifty miles.

And then, as suddenly as they had come, the shivers ceased and I felt an unearthly calm. I was neither hot nor cold now. The purity of the silence rang like a Buddhist bell, clear and endless. Here I was in the loneliest, emptiest place on earth, smiling inwardly, and on the outside utterly at peace, as if in some blissful limbo state between life and death.

The prattling, rather pathetic, panic-driven me who sees nothing but danger and desperation and occasionally even a premature demise in situations like this seemed to fade away into insignificance. He was replaced by a sense of utter certainty that everything was as it should be and that I was safe and that all I had to do was set off into the whiteness and I would be led to safety by something, someone inside me. A someone who always seems to hover around when I get myself into situations over which I have, and admit to myself that I have, no control whatsoever. I burst out laughing at the zaniness of the whole predicament, and my feet, without any prompting and guidance from the conscious part of me, walked me surely and certainly right back through the vast white silence to the jeep.

The Rann is still with me now. In times of silence I can return to its silence and in a strange way I find it comforting and reassuring. We all could possibly benefit from a Rann somewhere in our minds. A place of refuge and utter peace where, despite all evidence to the contrary, we are completely safe. A place in the mind, yet far, far beyond the mind.

> *I am going away to an unknown*
> *country where I shall have no past and no*
> *name, and where I shall be reborn again*
> *with a new face and an untied heart.*
> —COLLETTE

Love and Improvisation —A Périgord Interlude

The simple act of cooking can resonate across cultures and engage multitudes.

We had met by chance while I was wandering deep into France's cleft-and-canyon Périgord country and we liked one another immediately. So Pierre invited me back to his small but locally renowned restaurant and allowed me to join him at work in his kitchen. Apparently, it was quite an honor, according to his mother, a small, eagle-eyed, Piaf-like dynamo of a woman who watched every nuance of Pierre's preparation and cooking.

"He does not usually like strangers around when he is cooking."

"I understand," I said. "I'll stay in the corner and be very quiet."

She smiled through her warning scowls. It was actually quite a pleasant smile. But wary all the same. Nothing must disturb "the drama," as she called it, of Pierre's evening dinner performances. And nothing would. She would see to that.

So I sat on my stool in the corner. Pierre chatted briefly with me and described the offerings of the night: the foie gras with roasted chanterelles and a "marmalade" of "melted yellow peppers." I loved the expression "melted"—in my culinary dabblings I find it one of the most difficult of processes. Everything has to be done at a constant low temperature, but not too low, and the gentle stirring of the ingredients must also be virtually constant to prevent burning and to ensure the evenness of the soft, buttery *coulis* that emerge in an hour or so. And then, after a soup of pureed leeks, garlic, squash, and basil, he would prepare two main courses: great haunches of wild boar that had been marinating for two days in red Bordeaux wine, thyme, fennel, garlic, balsamic vinegar and, believe it or not, Jack Daniel's whiskey and would bake to mouthwatering succulence in a slow, even oven; and then something rather odd, a Japanese-style tempura of goose thigh pieces served with a Tunisian vegetable and couscous *tagine* and a sauce blended from goose drippings, lemongrass, coconut cream, ginger, and—I was surprised—his own mix of American Skippy peanut butter and Vietnamese fish sauce.

"That sounds like a Thai sauce—of sorts." I exclaimed.

Pierre smiled and nodded and said nothing.

"So—you're mixing Japanese, Tunisian, and Thai cuisines—all in one dish?"

"Of course," he replied.

"But what would your fellow Périgord chefs say to that? They seem to want to keep everything traditional, the way it's been done for centuries."

Pierre chuckled. "You are right. They do. And that is fine. But I don't."

"O.K."

"I travel you see. Very much. I close the restaurant for two long vacations and I go off to travel all over the world and meet other chefs and learn ideas from them and then I bring them back and see what happens here."

His smile and radiating enthusiasm were contagious.

"That's great. So Escoffier's not your only guru."

"Oh, he's in here too," said Pierre. "And Brillat-Savarin, Carême, Bocuse, Bruneau, Haeberlin, Troisgois, Boyer, Billoux, all the great chefs of France—past and present. I know them all. I've cooked with some of them. They're all here along with Nobu and many great New York and American chefs. And this week I celebrate the *tagines* of my Tunisian friend—not a chef, but an artist in Tunis, a lovely woman—and the sauce of a chef in a little restaurant in Phuket in a fishing village. It's not a tourist place, just a local place for the fishermen."

"So you're producing what—a kind of 'fusion' cooking?"

"Fusion? I don't like that word.

It sounds dangerous. Radioactive!" He gave me a great guffaw. His mother suddenly appeared at the kitchen door with a scowl. Maybe I was distracting her chef.

"Mama. He asks if I do 'fusion' cooking!"

"Poof!" she exclaimed, almost spitting. "*Merde!*"

He continued laughing and then explained. "No, not fusion. It is a bit of a bad word in the Périgord. I like to say 'inspirational' or 'improvisational.' I get together with all my chefs..." (I looked around the tiny restaurant. There were no other chefs. Two people were chopping and sautéing, one girl was working on elaborate desserts, and an old wrinkled man in the corner was doing something I couldn't quite comprehend with goose giblets)..."and we work together each night, we have fun, and see what we can concoct—improvise—from all the wonderful things I buy from my farmers, my suppliers."

"So the farmers are in this too?"

"Oh, but of course. They are—how you say—'partners' in what happens here. I know each one of them. I know who can grow the finest little vegetables—miniatures—the best peppers, the most perfect fennel, the richest purple basil. I work with them, spend time at their farms, sometimes I even dig the earth with them and help them plant things—don't I Mama?"

Mama was still at the door, scowling. Her English was limited so he translated. Then she stopped scowling and her face lit up in a beautiful smile that evaporated her wrinkles and transformed her normally down-turned mouth into the most loving of expressions. She said something softly in French. Pierre translated. "She says—my kitchen is so full of people I love that she can hardly squeeze in the door sometimes when I'm cooking!"

I looked around the kitchen, with its sparse array of assistants. "So—where are they?"

Another great guffaw. "*Stupide!*" he exclaimed. "They are not *here*," he said, stretching out his burly arms to encompass the whole kitchen. "They are *here!*" he shouted, placing both enormous hands on his head "and *here!*" both hands now on his huge chest, right over his heart.

His mother cracked up, as did the kitchen staff and even the old man in the corner with his giblets. They all tipped back their heads and the tiny kitchen was full of laughter and joy and all the wonderful fellowship that can exist between a small group of people intensely involved in one of life's most creative and satisfying activities—conceiving new dishes to please and nourish a clientele of equally exploratory eaters.

"It's packed in here," shouted Pierre between gasps. "All my friends—all the chefs I admire and love are here. And my mother, who taught me how to love food and fresh things. Her caring is in here too" (he hit his heart again with a great thump). "And my father," he pointed to the old man in the

corner, "he can't talk, he's had a stroke, but by God, he keeps me honest and excited. He knows exactly when I'm going a little too 'fusion'—too many ingredients, too many different flavors—and when I'm *really improvising*—when my friends and I are working together to create something truly unique. Truly special. A little nod from him" (he hit his heart again) "is better than a pat on the back from Paul [Bocuse]!"

℘

I'd intended to hang around Pierre's restaurant only for a day or so before disappearing into the canyons of the Dordogne—one of France's most dramatically scenic regions. But I changed my mind, or rather I changed my heart, and stayed on for almost a week, helping out where I could (I now know what Pierre's father was doing with those giblets but it's a restaurant secret—the secret to one of Pierre's greatest sauces—so that's all I can say), and watching and learning and watching and learning. Watching the magic of fresh creations every day—the blending of the new and the old, the outrageous and the traditional, the Orient with the Périgord—the blending of heart and mind—the blending of all the geniuses that fill Pierre's kitchen to overflowing every night.

And now my kitchen at home is crowded too. Whenever I'm in the "improv" mode, which is actually most days, I'm surrounded by Pierre and his coterie of colleagues and sous-chefs and all the great names in French and American cooking. They're all in there working with me, all combining their knowledge and love with my lowly efforts to create—not food really—but love, the love that comes from sharing myself (and my newfound Périgord friends) with those I love through the magic of cooking and the creation of unique dishes that come from the heart (big chest-thump here à la Pierre).

REFLECTIONS

The Tree

I know this back road. Same somewhere. Sometime. There's a twist ahead I think. By a small bridge. Lopsided. Looks like it'll collapse any minute but the buttress has a date carved in it that says...wait for it...here it comes. It says... A.D. 1619. Well—I guess it's O.K. for a while longer.

Why do I know this back road? I was here with some-one years ago. Someone I didn't know too well but who, over the course of a few days, taught me so much. I remem-ber just listening to his soft voice. But who was he? I can almost see his face. A beard? Did he have a beard or was he going to grow one? He said he liked mine, and he talked so much about his travels, his family, his varied lives as a baker, chauffeur, chef, teacher, a whole rainbow of interests and skills, and as an illustrator. Children's books mainly, I think.

The track spools out ahead of me, curling downhill now through deep woods dappled with sunlight that flares the fall colors into sudden explosions of brilliant maple scarlets, alder golds, and the deep bronzes of the sycamores and ash. And then suddenly I'm in a broad valley with emerald green meadows, a curling stream, sparkling and chittering in quicksilver flashes, and a tree.

That tree...

Of course—the tree we'd sketched together. You were using it for some children's book about the forest; I was wondering if it might work as an illustration for the title page of one of my books.

James! James! That's you my friend. My fleeting friend of years ago. A friend who was gone so fast. I'd hardly said hello when that ghastly letter came from your wife...your death...climbing somewhere. Austria was it? Australia? I'd blocked it. I'd buried you just as you were buried in your village by that church where I met your wife for the first time, and your two children.

And now you're back with me James. I'm sorry I was such a coward for so long. I meant to meet with you again when the grief was gone. But it took until today. Until this tree...which I'm sketching now James. With you at my side. Just for you I'm sketching this tree again. And you're talk-ing and I can remember your descriptions of the Sahara, and the Seychelles, and your hike, like mine, up the Pennine Way—up the spine of Britain. I can remember everything. And now it's hard to tell the difference between what I remember and what I hear you saying now. And yes, oh boy! I miss you too. But now I see—you were here all the time. I just forgot for a while, that's all. But now I won't. You're here to stay, my friend. You're part of me again now.

So James, you think this sketch is coming along O.K.?

Almost Gone #5 —Perils in the Pine Barrens

Try to understand the root of your fear—it is an excellent teacher.

My car seemed to know exactly where it was going on that lovely warm afternoon, deep into the wild Pine Barrens of southern New Jersey. This vast million-acre expanse of forest, lakes, winding "cedar-water" brown rivers is a place full of strange tales of its reclusive inhabitants, the Pineys, and even a legendary monster, the New Jersey Devil, apparently an unpleasantly avaricious creature with a horse's head, horns, a dragon's tail, and a penchant for eating anything and everything that gets in its way.

It was as though my little Toyota were driving itself on those sinuating sand trails through the deep and shadowed forest. I just sat there and breathed deeply in resin-scented breezes. I knew I'd be leaving in two days for weeks of travel—all over the world—new people, new experiences, new adventures, wherever I wanted to go. I was on a rolling high. Everything was in synch. This was the moment I'd wanted, I'd needed, before I left on my real journey. Me and my life and the beauty of everything around me, all together in total harmony. Great!

Damn!

I'm told these moments of truth and harmony are often fleeting. Very necessary, very satisfying, but short-lived. Well, this one was practically stillborn. One moment I was soaring high as a hawk, gliding in the utter freedom of the moment. Next, my car was leaning at a crazy angle, stuck axle deep in a black bog at the side of the track. I had taken—correction—my car, in which I'd placed total trust, had taken one of the wriggles in the track too quickly and had skidded on the loose sand into this pernicious patch of swamp, hardly visible in the gloomy shadows. The driver's side was deep in goo. I peered out the side window and saw the mud bubbling like a slow-boiling cauldron. The passenger's side was still over sand and I managed to squirm out like a snail from its shell.

I had no idea where I was. I'd no recall of how long I'd been in my little reverie, but I knew I'd driven miles and miles on that track, taking forks at will, becoming gleefully—intentionally—lost. Walking back to the main road would take hours (if I could ever find it), and it was already late afternoon. Obviously I had to find a way of getting the car out of the swamp by myself.

I'd been in similar situations before. I knew all the tricks—sliding something solid under the stuck wheel, letting the clutch in slow, getting a firm grip, and—zip—you're out. All desert travelers tell you about their experiences in soft sand and suchlike. They always seem to live to tell the tales, with appropriate authorial embellishments of course. And I felt as cocky as they. A couple of well-placed planks in the goo and I'd be off again.

Unfortunately, I hadn't brought any planks with me, or anything else of use for that matter. So I ambled off into the gloom to find dead pine branches to simulate my nonexistent planks. Pretty soon I'd managed to shove quite a pile of debris under the offending rear wheel. Seemed nice and firm. Well done, son. (I allowed myself a little complacency.) This guy sure knows his sticky-situation stuff.

I was back in the driver's seat like a snail in rapid reverse. A gentle roll of the engine, into first gear, gently release the clutch until you feel the grip of the wheel.

And...glop!

The swamp sounded like a ravenous whale about to swallow me, clutch, trunk, and fender. Slurp, goo, and glop. Great lumps of mud were flying everywhere and then the back end suddenly sank another foot into the swamp. Not at all the way desert ramblers do it. A right regal cock-up.

Now I had to climb steeply upward out of the passenger's side and jump down to solid earth. The front passenger-side wheel was stuck a foot in the air. The mud was already over the tailpipe and part of the rear fender. Now I was well and truly stuck.

And right on cue, the mosquitoes found me. It was now early evening and the light was getting dusky. And here was this sweet-blooded, muddied human just standing around chomping and cursing and making an ideal happy-hour snack. And did they snack. Far more aggressively than their Alaskan counterparts or the dreaded North Woods terrors, buzzing, swooping, plunging their proboscises into every exposed inch of my flesh.

Obviously I would have to find the main road twelve, maybe twenty, miles back. In all that distance I'd not seen any other vehicle or human being. Not even a shack. Nothing but sand, pines, and blood-mad mosquitoes.

The situation had lost all its romance. For the first time in a long time I felt scared, stuck in the middle of this New Jersey wilderness, awaiting the wail of the dreaded Jersey Devil or, worse still, a visit from the Pineys themselves. Their sinister reputation is not all myth. People vanish forever in these parts. Only a few weeks prior I'd read of a body discovered deep in the Barrens. It had been there for months and was in six distinct pieces, placed precisely around a fifteen-foot circle. (Have you noticed how your brain loves to bring back useless fragments of data at the worst possible moments?)

The silence deepened. Even the mosquitoes seemed to lose interest in me now (maybe fear gives off a special antimosquito vibration?). No breezes blew and the light was deep gloom, dead gray actually. I was reluctant to leave the car. I had no food or water. What I did have was an enormous twenty-pound bag full of my cameras, lenses and all that professional traveler stuff I was not about to leave behind.

I unloaded as much as I could, locked all the doors and prepared myself for a long hike. Then Anne suddenly came to mind. She would be worried. I thought of her looking anxiously out from our Philadelphia apartment window (from the twenty-seventh floor of our tower you could almost see the edge of the Pine Barrens, a mere twenty miles or so east of the city). She would be telling herself that everything was O.K. I had to find a phone, I thought, and then managed a bit of a smile—I had to find myself first.

I set off at a good pace, back along the track that possessed none of its previous enticements now. Odd rustlings came from the dark forest. Occasional grunts and throaty growls. I started to walk faster. Then something else. Like a growl but different. And getting louder. Way back down the track near the car. Then flashes through the trees. Very faint at first, like glowworms, but getting brighter.

A car, a truck, a real live human being? I could see the lights quite plainly now, flickering through the trees, and hear the welcome roar of an engine. Engines? Yes, definitely more than one engine. Wonderful! See, I admonished myself, all you need is a bit of luck and faith. After all, you've always managed somehow to get out of every scrape you've ever been in. Saved by my guardian angel once again. Thank you!

I hurried back toward the car, lugging my bag of cameras. Yes, there were lights, lots of them. And they were stopped. Engines were roaring. I had a piece of old rope in the trunk. Bit of a pull and everything would be just fine again. I'd even be home in time for dinner. The cats would be so delighted to see me. Anne would listen enthralled to my tales and we'd drink champagne and have a good laugh at my predicament and groundless fears.

I could make out three bikes by the car—big Harley-Davidson creatures each with three balloon-type tires for sand travel. People were moving around. All of the bikes had large containers on the back with metal things sticking out. I came closer half running and then slowed down. The metal things sticking out were guns—enormous shotguns and rifles. Also, shovels. And pickaxes. And the people didn't look right. In the bright beams from the bikes I could see long hair tied with bandannas, leather jackets trimmed with rivets and spikes, mud-caked jeans, and enormous laced boots with metal toe caps.

Hell's Angels? Or something worse?

"Hi!" I tried to sound nonchalant and cheerful.

No one replied. Not one of the three enormous men even looked at me. A young girl, also encased in black leather, stood off to the side, leg on the upturned wheel of my car.

They were laughing. Nasty sly chuckles. One of the men was mumbling something low in a gravelly bass voice and they all sniggered again.

"Thought I'd never find anybody round here," I said (I could hear my voice rising unnaturally and cracking).

Still no response. No acknowledgment that I even existed. Then one of the men turned slowly, the apparent leader of the bunch, and looked toward me but not at me. I traced his gaze. He was staring straight at my camera bag. I had so much equipment inside that I hadn't been able to close the zipper. My expensive Nikons with fancy lenses gleamed in the beams of their lights. He growled something to his companions and they all turned and stared at the bag and smiled some of the nastiest smiles I've ever seen. The girl gave a hissing giggle and I didn't like the sound at all. So this is how it happens, I thought (sometimes I wish my brain would just switch off), at night, stuck in the Pines, helpless, with a pack of Pineys, armed, eyeballing a couple thousand dollars of easy pickings. And another hapless back-roader vanishes forever.

"Can you help me get this thing out?" I asked. "I'm stuck." (Talk about the bleedin' obvious).

More gravelly sniggers. Still no one looked at me. Then one of the men slowly sauntered over to the car and rocked it. I could hear the bog gurgle. More chuckles. Then, as if they did this kind of thing all the time, two of the men moved to the rear, one moved to the front (the girl still giggling), gave a quick heave in which they lifted the whole damned machine (half a ton of mulchy, muddy metal) and dropped it with a bounce back in the middle of the sand track. All in a second or two. Easy as cutting cake. I stood gaping.

"Well—thanks. Thanks a lot. Thank you." I muttered on. Now they all stood, arms in riveted belts and stared—right at me—with those sinister smirks.

"Get in." The largest man with the longest hair was speaking.

"Right. Right. I'll see if she's O.K. There's plenty of mud around the tailpipe."

I squeezed between them (like passing through a granite wall) and slid into the driver's seat. She started! First go. Ah—what a machine! "Thanks again," I said breathlessly, "I'll just get her turned around and…"

"You'll never make it that way." The big one again. But I felt safer now inside my car with the doors locked from the inside.

"Oh, don't worry. I'll find it."

"Follow this guy." He pointed to one of his companions who was already mounting his bike and revving the engine. That girl was still watching and smirking. She really unnerved me. Like a bloodthirsty Madame Defarge with a front seat at the guillotine.

"We'll be right behind." They were already lining up their bikes.

"Where are we going?"

"Faster way out."

Oh yeah. Sure. Right to some broken-down shack in the darkest part of the pines for some ritual satanic sacrifice. Me! Bye-bye sweet life.

"Listen…" I began.

"Let's go!"

They literally corralled my car forward, deeper and deeper down the track, which now rapidly became a rutted trail with more swampy patches. It was black dark now. I needed full beams to avoid overhanging branches and rocks half hidden in the sand.

Pretty soon there was hardly any track at all, just snaky patches of flattened earth. How stupid could I be? Like the metaphoric lamb to the slaughter. They were still going fast, not giving me a chance to slow down and think. Then ahead was water, a stretch of shallow swamp. The lead bike spurred through. I skidded and swirled about but somehow made it. Branches were crashing against my windshield. Mud sprayed high on both sides. I couldn't see any signs of trail now.

O.K. Time for action, David, Rambo-style. These guys aren't ever going to let me out of this damned wilderness. At least make a break for it. Give it your best shot. Put your foot down, get ahead of the front guy and try to blast your way out. They're going to get you anyway. At least go down fighting.

Waiting…waiting for a chance to break. The track is widening again. I can get past. I can see tire ruts ahead. Maybe I've got a real chance after all.

Foot down, fist on horn, lights full beam, and we're off; the car leaps ahead like a leopard, missing the front biker by inches, sand hissing on the chassis. A surge of pure beautiful speed, barreling down the track, the bike lights behind me now. Oh boy, I'm going to make it, I'm going to get out alive.

Then the track ends. With no warning. I slam everything on, including the hand brake, and the machine spins in an explosion of flying pebbles and sand. This is it! I thought I'd won but now I've had it.

And then…an enormous eighteen-wheeler roars past, ten feet from my front fender. Three cars follow, flashing past in flurries of hot air. There are lights. A lot of them. It's a *high-way*! A real hard-surface, macadam, fast-lane, beautiful, flat, straight, smooth highway.

Someone hammers at my window. It's the big man with the longest hair. His bandanna is halfway down his eyes and he's as mad as hell. "What the motherf— hell do you think you're doing you crazy motherf— b—, you're out of your f— mind, you stupid son-of-a-….!"

I couldn't think of anything to say or do except smile as nicely as I could. I was safe and that was enough.

The two other bikers strolled up and peered in—dirty, frazzled, young-old faces looking at me as if I'd gone wacko.

Then one of them gave that smile again. "Bet you thought you'd never make it out."

I still couldn't speak. I just nodded like the crazy man they thought I was. The big man was still mother-f—g away in the background and I could hear the girl giggling again. One remained at my window with an expression I took to be of amused empathy.

I lowered the window a fraction. "Look," I said, my adrenaline still scouring through my system and my heart beating to a staccato-techno beat, "I'm sorry about that...y'see I thought..."

"That's O.K. I know what you thought. I know those Piney stories too. We scared the livin' b'jesus out a'you—right?"

"Right."

"Make you crap in your pants, right?"

"Almost."

"Right. Well I've been there, too."

"Why, what happened?"

"Aw nuthin'—it was a long while back. But when I saw your face I knew what you was thinkin'! Hell you could have been me a few years back. You almost made *me* crap in my pants you looked so damned scared!"

"Yes—well...I was."

"Well, don't feel so bad. You're safe now. We've all got demons." He leaned closer so the others couldn't hear him. "Listen, y'think these leather outfits and rivets and big-mother-f—r bikes makes us different? It's all show. It's fun, but it's all show. We all know what's underneath, and it's the same for you and me and every guy I've ever met. Sometimes it's just a bit deeper under the surface, but it's there, always. We all got that in common—our bogeymen."

"Yes" I said, calming and looking the biker right in the eye. "You're dead right. Thank you."

"Well—you're O.K. now—so—look, turn right here and it takes you straight into Philly."

"Great. And again, thank you."

"You're O.K. Get movin'. I'll straighten it with the guys. Hey, and listen," he said, moving closer again. "Dump the bogeymen—y'don't need 'em. S'like my dad said when he died, 'Life's too short. Fear nothing.'"

And that was it. They were gone. Bikes revving like a hundred hornets' nests, lights disappearing down the track back into the forest, and then utter silence.

I got out of the car and put one foot on the hard—beautifully hard—road. It felt wonderful. "Turn right and it takes you straight into Philly," he said. So I did.

And "dump the bogeymen," he said.

So I tried to do that too...but, as I've found out many times since in my wanderings, you never quite lose them. They just hide away deeper...waiting.

True travel...is a profound desire to be other than what one seems to be.
—OCTAVIO PAZ

The Temptations of a Tanka

*If you are open to it, the essence
of a master can seep in.*

Nepal's capital city, Kathmandu, is one of the world's most intriguing places. This tiny mountain-bound land of magic and mystery is seductive in the extreme. Centuries of slow, isolated cultural development here have produced a beguiling mélange of architectural forms, spiritual intensity, and social richness, undoubtedly unique on earth. Just as I was, outsiders are often overwhelmed by the power of the place, a place offering itself as a touchstone for those eternal values and truths that Western nations have often forgotten in their wild pursuit of wealth and material abundance. Of course Nepalis also chase wealth, as do people everywhere, but here the teachers are more often the taught. It comes with the territory.

I was staying with a couple of friends in the center of Kathmandu, both involved as I am from time to time with my wife's work with the blind. They had entertained me royally, and I remember one afternoon in particular when the three of us sat drinking *chhang* (the local home-brewed millet beer) served from a communal bowl in the shady garden of a restaurant famous for its Tibetan wontons, or *momos*. We had gorged our way into a pleasantly loopy state. Over the garden wall I could hear the spinning of prayer wheels in a temple courtyard. A flock of white pigeons curled over our heads. The ceaseless prattle of the city seemed a long way away.

"I'd like you to meet an artist," the girl said, filling my glass with *chhang* for the umpteenth time.

"Lovely," I said. I had no special plans. Kathmandu does that to you. Time becomes seductively elastic and nothing seems particularly urgent in this lovely rice-paddied valley under the soaring, snow-sheened mountains.

Eventually the three of us finished the bowl, and she led the way past the temple and into a monastery at the end of a muddy track. We were greeted by monks in orange robes and, after a whispered conversation, led to a small cell at the rear of the compound. And there he was, a tiny elfin creature sitting on a stool in a bare room furnished only with a bed and an old wooden chest. A single bulb hung down on a frayed wire from the ceiling.

He turned and smiled, and the room seemed immediately brighter. It was a smile I shall always remember. His whole face shone, his eyes sparkled and seemed translucent; I felt as if I'd been immersed in warm, silky water. We were all smiling. I looked at my friends and their faces shone. The whole room was one big grin.

The girl introduced him to me, but I've long forgotten his name. It doesn't matter anyway. I was mesmerized by him. His aura was almost tangible, evoking stillness and joy and something far, far deeper.

"He's from the Dolpo," she said.

Now, like many of the ancient Himalayan kingdoms that once existed all along the Himalayan range, Dolpo is still a remote and unexplored region, three hundred miles or so to the west of Kathmandu.

"How did he get here?"

"He walked."

Of course. Even Nepal's major road, the "Rajpath" to India, one of the most tortuous mountain roads in the world (and one I was to experience firsthand later), was completed only in 1959. Most of the country is still roadless, bound together only by spiderweb networks of narrow paths.

"That must have taken quite a while."

"Three weeks."

"Alone?"

"Oh no," she laughed. "He is a very famous artist in the Dolpo. Two hundred of his followers came with him."

"Why did he come?" I asked.

"He was invited to paint a series of *tankas* for the temple here."

Now, *tankas* (or *thangkas*) are one of the major art forms of Nepal's strange blending of Buddhist and Hindu faiths. They are illustrated records, usually composed in circular mandala form, depicting the lives, deeds and incarnations of the various deities and the supreme power of Brahma, the metaphysical absolute, the beginning and the end. They are works of the most exquisite detail painted with tiny brushes and using natural dyes made from cinnabar, lapis lazuli, flower petals, and gold dust. While the broad themes are constant, artists are given freedom to interpret all the various facets of Buddhism's four truths—pain, suffering, desire, and nirvana—and all the entangled attributes and activities of the deities—erotic, comic, cruel, demonic, loving, and lethargic (the gods are often appealingly human in their foibles).

The result is a staggeringly rich panoply of images, pulsing with life—an artwork of great beauty and subtlety but also an important visual aid to meditation and religious insight.

The smiling artist said something in a soft, singsong voice.

"He's asking if you'd like to see one of his *tankas*."

"Yes, I would, very much."

The elfin man nodded, opened up the wooden chest in the corner of his cell and carefully lifted out a rectangle of stretched canvas about four feet high and three feet wide.

Slowly, almost shyly, he turned the canvas toward us.

The room exploded with color—bright emerald-green mountains, golden-edged clouds, pink and sapphire-blue lotus blossoms, curling traceries of leaves, haloed gods—some black and fierce, some with elephants' faces, others with huge mouths and horns and a welter of gracefully waving arms, some almost transparent with long-fingered upraised palms and gentle almond-shaped eyes, and all clad in meticulously detailed robes. There were scores of separate images, each one tingling with symbolic gestures I couldn't begin to comprehend. And yet the painting possessed a swirling unity of composition so that each detail could be enjoyed separately and yet still form an integral part of the whole. Far more structured than the rambling fantasies of Hieronymus Bosch, but just as filled with life and movement—and humanity. These were gods, but gods reflecting the kaleidoscopic miasma of human experience and knowledge.

My friends had seen *tankas* before, hundreds of them (you can buy ones of questionable quality throughout Kathmandu), but even they were silenced by the power and vitality of this little artist's work.

"How long?" I began.

The girl asked how long the *tanka* had taken to paint.

"He says about three months—three months of twelve-hour days."

"And he's painting more?"

"Six. He's been asked to do six."

"And then?"

"He'll go back to Dolpo."

"Walking?"

"Walking."

"Three hundred miles."

"Right. Three hundred miles."

"And when he gets back?"

"He'll paint more *tankas*. This is his life."

I had no more questions. The little man was no longer "little"; his presence filled each of us in turn. Then the artist smiled at us, slowly turned to his table in the corner, lit a lamp and pulled back an old woven cloth to reveal the beginning of yet another *tanka*. He began to work with a brush so devoid of hairs it seemed to float above the canvas, painting as if by magic. On closer inspection I saw it had eight, maybe ten, tiny strands of hair, barely visible even from a couple of feet away. He was painting a lotus blossom, less than a quarter of an inch around and yet meticulous in every detail.

I continued to watch his brush, almost hypnotized by its slow, steady movements and the enticing emergence of the white petals of the lotus. Maybe I *was* hypnotized (it's happened before) because looking back I'm still not really certain what happened next except, although I was sitting beside him— a separate entity—I felt to be slowly entering him, his mind, his seeing, his breathing (very soft and regular—not the held breath and sudden furious gulps of air that I tend to take when I'm painting) and in some strange way, entering his whole life. I experienced part of his long walk from the Dolpo and then back again (no pain, just the hazy continuity of it all). His followers were behind him, all walking as if of one mind, a single living entity rather than two hundred distinct individuals. I sensed the flow of his walk ease into this tiny room like ripples and its continuance through the flow of the brush and the emergence of all the hundreds of images on the *tanka,* and the next *tanka* and the next…in an endless round of complete certainty and creation.

My friends had to virtually lift me out of the room. They thanked him profusely. I didn't want to leave. I felt I was leaving something behind. Something I needed. Something vital. I was tempted to stay there, just sitting beside him—in him—but my friends obviously thought otherwise. As we moved toward the door he reached out his right hand—smooth-skinned and long-fingered—and held it an inch or so above my out-stretched hand. I felt a sudden jolt of enormous power that filled my whole body with energy. His smile was warming my shoulders as we left and then I slowly realized, through the glow in my head and chest, that I hadn't left *me* behind. He had left *himself* behind—in me.

And he has remained with me, clear and utterly tangible, since that day. And sometime in the future, when I feel I understand enough, and when he nudges me inside and offers to be my teacher, I may even begin to learn to paint my own *tanka.*

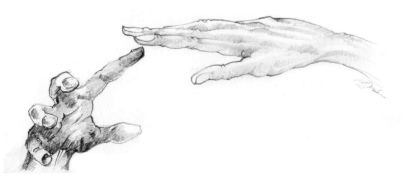

REFLECTIONS

An Absolute Disaster

A total loss! No other words to describe it. The kind of thing all writers dread. The sudden loss of a manuscript—this book's manuscript! All of it. Drafts, disks, computer—all vanished as a result of one small, stupid act of carelessness. My carelessness.

I'd left the damned car unlocked. I guess I got complacent. I was on my way to a cabin in upstate New York—yes, a real cabin with stone fireplace, wood-burning stove, the lot—and deep, deep in the deepest woods. I needed a few days to give the manuscript a final reading, tweak the tales a little, hone the edges, and generally prepare this work—a distillation of years of travel and exploration—for publication. Then it would be released to (I hoped) a needy world that would embrace its perspectives on life and redefine our purpose here on this lonely blue ball floating in infinity, bring new joys in living...well, you get the idea—you're reading the book!

But apparently someone's own personal needs supersed-
ed that of the world in general. Someone in the city where
I'd parked the car needed it urgently, not for nurture, or
insight, or to kick open a few doors of perception and fresh
possibilities, but rather to sell (the computer, not the book.
The book would of course be utterly irrelevant) for a quick
fix or two in a life that was fixed to the max and where all
new ideas and explorations and revelations had long since
ceased.

As you might imagine I went through about a dozen
selves in the first couple of minutes following my discovery
of the theft—furious anger at the thief, loathing of the cal-
lous disinterest of the Creator and the universe in general,
self-loathing for my naiveté and stupidity (of course things
get stolen from an unlocked car in the city, you dumb idiot),
ready to kill, plans to post huge rewards on sky-high bill-
boards, rampaging through every ghetto alley to find my
disks, etc., etc.

I was a fragmented mess—screaming, raging, weeping,
cursing, plotting, threatening, and wishing I knew more
about the mechanics of bloody vendettas or how to hire a
host of hit men. I was a series of someones I'd never known
well before, gruesome selves that I'd rarely met were slither-
ing out of my psyche and vowing to destroy everything
around them, and then...

...and then I woke up.

And I realized in a great gush of joy and relief that it
was all a horrible dream—a nightmare of total nihilism—
and that the manuscript and disks and computer were all
safely sitting on my desk across the room and the smell of
fresh-brewed coffee was wafting up the stairs from the

kitchen where Anne was already up and petering about in that beautiful bright dawn light, getting ready for our sojourn in the log cabin in those deep, deep woods.

*And then, as the terrors subsided, an idea came for the perfect sequel to this book...an obvious idea...*Our Dream-Selves—Far Stranger Adventures and Explorations!

Burn Your Boats

Burn your boats
and sink your ships
and blow your bridges high
—You've nothing to lose
nothing to choose
nothing—except
to fly!

I Am Amazonia

You can expand your soul by absorbing
a piece of the landscape.

"There's just too much of it...too much!" said the large lady sitting next to me on the plane.

"Too much of what?" I asked.

"Land. Forest. You know—all this!" She wavered her plump fingers about and imperiously pointed out the window.

She'd got the window seat I'd wanted. The flight was full, a real sardiner, so I had to grumpily submit to an aisle seat, where your knees are banged by the toilet-trotters, drink trolleys, and kids playing Sitting Bull and Custer up and down that ridiculously narrow aisle (does it really cost more to build a fatter plane?).

"It's the Amazon Basin," I said. "It's big." We'd left Bolivia's Santa Cruz airport an hour or so ago having had a spectacular flight over the Andes Cordillera, with their razor peaks and shattered ridges and vast ice fields and glaciers.

"But it's all the same," she responded. "Jungle, jungle, and more jungle!"

"Listen," I suggested tentatively. "Why don't we switch seats? You can stretch out a bit more [liar] and that sunlight won't be in your eyes all the time [max-out smarmy stuff here]."

So—we did. And, for me, that was it for the rest of the flight. Forget the food and drinks and offers of cushions and rugs. Everyone else was going to sleep, apparently oblivious to the incredible vistas from the windows. Blinds were being pulled down and the torpor of travel-slumberers was about to begin.

But not for me.

My blind stayed well and truly up for the whole of that magnificent three-hour flight from south to north across northern Bolivia, the whole of Brazil, and into the "reclaimed" land of southern Venezuela. Across the unbelievable vastness of mighty Amazonia—a region more than half the size of the USA. An experience I shall carry with me into oblivion.

And what did I see, you might ask?

Well—my portly companion had been absolutely right. There certainly was an awful lot of jungle down there. Infinite blue-green blankets of it with geography-lesson tangles of oxbowing rivers cutting sinewy silt and torrent paths through the wilderness. Utter wilderness. Nothing I've ever seen anywhere in all my world travels could prepare me for this sense of endless wild space unmolested by any visible intruders—just a great and beautiful melding of forest and river, river and forest, forest and river.... And in the far, far distance, hundreds of miles to the west, I could just make out the cloud line along the crest of the Andes themselves, that gigantic 4,000 mile-long spine of South America. And it was curved! Very slightly, from end to end, a slow curve of the cloud line reflecting the curve of the earth itself.

Now, I have been in Amazonia. On the ground. In the jungle. I have suffered the curses of endless biting flies, sweltering sauna-bath heat, mud up to my crotch (and occasionally higher). I have hacked away in machete-madness trying to carve out the semblance of a path through almost impenetrable scrub laced with enormous spiderwebs and serpentining vines that seem to want to grab you and squeeze the juicy life out of your every orifice. And I've also avoided bathing in the rivers renowned for piranha and anacondas (the film of the same name was only a *slight* exaggeration) and those ghastly little wormy things whose only purpose in life seems to be to creep up into your extremely personal orifices and spread out their pernicious little spines and lock themselves in place until you go mad with pain and have to have them surgically removed at great and permanent damage to your lower intestinal tract. Oh yes, I've definitely been there and done that. And quite frankly, although adventuring is my life, I have no desire whatsoever to go back.

But from this height, from my martini-hazed vantage point (yes, I finally did give in to the persistent hostess and her cart of alcoholic delights), Amazonia seems to be a benign—almost sublime—place. Just lying there, spongy-textured with rainforest, unmolested, untrammeled, she seems creaturelike, a living, soft-breathing entity that absorbs the crud of our despoiled air and gives back great and generous sighs of life-giving oxygen that are carried by currents across the enormous continent of South America and on around our globe, nurturing other forests, mountain ranges, vast plains, cities—and ultimately, each one of us.

Once in a while I spot a clearing, a minute ragged circle of open land the size of a nail head, dotted with tiny huts and what appears to be little gardens. Some small tribal group has made its home there. And in that little community are doubtless dogs, pigs, kids bawling and breast-feeding, men with bows and arrows and spears. They possibly believe they're alone in this vast greenness—alone on the whole planet (if they know there are such things as planets). They'll have their demons, and tales of terror and folklore, and mores and gods. Maybe they think our plane is one of them—a silver bird-god with motionless wings leaving a thin white linear cloud behind itself high up in the bluer-than-blue sky. Maybe they measure their days by the plane-bird's regular passing...and maybe they know all we know and much, much more...timeless wisdoms which we have long forgotten...

And then it's gone. The clearing, the families, the children, all vanished into the soft heat haze hanging shroudlike over the forest that once again resumes its untouched wholeness.

Another river comes spooling, its waters a rich tan color of silt and sand. Nothing moves on the river—no boats, no signs of life—just that endless slow bending and winding that has been the river's story for millions upon millions of years.

But maybe it's all a magnificent illusion. Although I can't see it from my westward-looking side of the plane I know that Gerald Durrell was right when he wrote:

> These great ecosystems (of the rainforest) are like complex tapestries. A million complicated threads, interwoven, make up the whole picture...but what nature cannot cope with is the steady undermining of its fabric by the activities of man.

By its very nature the tropical rainforest is the richest, most diverse, and most complex biome on the planet and also the least understood by science. These magnificent powerhouses of nature—wet, dense, humid, multilayered, canopied tumults of rapid growth and decomposition—still remain enticingly elusive. Their capacities for efficient nutrient-recycling, constant rejuvenation, and the intimate melding of hundreds of plant species—from 200-foot-high buttressed giants festooned with epiphytes, orchids, lianas, mosses, and lichens, to low-light understories of ferns, shrubs, saplings, and ground-hugging plants—make tropical rain forests by far the most productive vegetation systems on earth. Along with the thousands of species of birds, mammals, reptiles, butterflies, and insects beyond number that cohabit in the canopies, nature created an almost miraculous blending of ecosystems here linked by complex food chains in which all forest organisms are dependant upon one another for mutual survival.

And yet, and yet. Almost half of the tropical rain forest, that eons ago covered more than 6 million square miles of our earth, has already been destroyed, and the rate of deforestation between 1980 and 1990 in Amazonia alone was almost double that of the previous decade—something approaching 58,000 square miles per year (an area larger than the whole of New York state). Threats are multitudinous—the most severe being logging, slash-and-burn activities for new (but weak soil) farmland and cattle ranges, mining, pollution, hydro-electric schemes, and a dozen other plagues—all driven by the great unstoppable engines of human population increase and spiraling consumer demands. The predicted impact of this destruction is almost too dramatic to contemplate: violent climatic changes; vastly reduced oxygen-production; increased carbon dioxide in the atmosphere (the oft-discussed "greenhouse effect"); extinction of fragile indigenous cultures; and elimination of vast, untapped resources for food and medicine.

"So—is it interesting then?" asked my ample female neighbor sleepily.

"Yes," was all I could think to say. "It's unbelievably beautiful."

She yawned, "But it's all the same."

I smiled, "Yes—it is. And hopefully it'll stay just that way."

We were now well into the third hour of flight—that's three hours at more than 500 miles per hour—and still the forest went on and on. I wanted to see some of the destruction. I wanted to feel my anger at such despoliation and the urgency of our need to put a stop to our own mindless madness. Maybe on the other side of the plane, looking east toward the coastal lowlands, there might be another story.

So go and look, part of me said. Go and see for yourself.

But I didn't. I was just happy enough to know that, from my vantage point at least, it all appeared endless green (far more than I'd ever imagined from all the doom and gloom hyperbole I'd ingested), and scrolling rivers and more green fading into hazy infinities. An immensity almost beyond comprehension. A mind-bending and magnificent monotony—this huge and beautiful thing, breathing, living an oh-so-complex, oh-so-timeless existence. I wanted to thank it for being so big and intact and pristine; I wanted to reach out and stroke it, caress it. More than that—I wanted to absorb it, to make it a part of me, to become a part of all its vastness and richness and power.

And in my mind, I did, and remembered the warning in a fragment of a poem or a song I'd heard long, long ago:

> Once I had mountains in the palm of my hand
> And rivers ran through it every day
> I must have been mad
> I never knew what I had
> Until I threw it all away

Well, there'd be no throwing away in this instance, I promised myself.

And so that's how, in the very odd and mysterious way that minds and spirits seem to work, I absorbed something of the essence of this amazing place within me and...became a part of Amazonia.

A Wonderful Wacky Weekend

*Your wildest adventures can happen without
ever leaving home.*

It was all planned. Weeks of brochures, price comparisons, schedules, bookings, lists, and more lists. Papayas and palm trees, mangoes and moonlight strolls, lobsters, lobsters, lobsters. A long weekend on a Caribbean island.

Wonderful!

Then something happened.

"Darling," she said (slowly, with feeling—always a danger sign). "Isn't it a wee bit expensive for a weekend? After all, as soon as we're unpacked we'll be packing again."

"Yes, but..."

"And they told us it rains every afternoon."

"Yes, but..."

"And didn't they warn us about..."

End of discussion.

Instead we created what is bound to become a time-honored tradition: the WWW—the Wonderful Wacky Weekend. Three days of all the best gourmet foods we've always wanted to try, the best wines, a big box of crazy-priced chocolates, music we've never *really* listened to, fantastic recipes to cook together, and a savings of hundreds of dollars to top it all off!

We canceled everything and made the living room the focus of our first WWW. But it was the wrong mood: too bright, too cluttered with furniture.

"A desert tent," I said.

She agreed.

So a desert tent it was: king-size mattress dragged from the bedroom, pillows and cushions everywhere, blinds down for a soft-filtered, dusky light, candles, incense. The tent itself was a huge Indonesian cloth (a beautiful wedding present, never used) suspended from the ceiling light and tied by red ribbons to the walls. You had to crawl in and out. The space inside curved down and then slightly up at the edges in soft folds—it truly felt like a tent, an Arabian Nights fantasy. The mood inside was exotic and erotic, with purples, indigos, and scarlets glowing in gentle light. The two cats loved it.

We stopped work early after Friday lunch and went shopping: a large silver and blue tin of Beluga Malossol caviar; four superb pâtés (two soft and velvety and two country-chunky); wafer-thin Parma prosciutto, German Westphalia ham, three types of Italian salami; cheeses galore (including a superbly soft Italian Gorgonzola and a wheel of French triple-crème Explorateur); a whole gamey pheasant; Scottish smoked salmon; escargots; a box of Docetti Delicati; three types of coffee beans; sheets of dried seaweed for sushi; homemade pastas; five varieties of fresh mushrooms; exotic salad ingredients we'd only read about in magazines; Kalamata Greek olives; pineapples, mangoes, and papayas; clusters of fresh asparagus; one whole black truffle cushioned in a glass vial; crisp loaves of fresh Italian and French breads still warm from the oven—and two huge lobsters, of course. All this and some of the most extravagant champagnes and wines we could find—a panoply of overt hedonism for barely a third of what we'd planned to spend on that ridiculous four-day Caribbean jaunt!

We entered our retreat and carefully laid the delicacies on our glass coffee table (the one with the chip on the corner), disguised with my grandmother's hand-crocheted cloths. We lit incense sticks, put on a quiet tape of bamboo flute music, took the phone off the hook, locked all the doors, removed all clocks and watches.

At last look it was 6:15 on Friday evening. Our first WWW was in session.

We had no real idea what we planned to do or what outcomes we expected. We decided to let things happen as they happened, timelessly—to nibble when we felt like nibbling, talk when the mood struck, sleep when we were sleepy.

We began with the Debussy and the caviar—fat bubbles bursting with salt-fishy pungency—washed down with tiny glasses of vodka (the vodka bottle frozen in a solid block of ice with two full-petaled daisies inside the ice), and us, sprawled in our tent, bathed in that soft, beautiful music.

Then we read fragments of works we hadn't touched for years: Tolstoy, Steinbeck, Wordsworth, Frost, Hardy, Thoreau (no speed reading permitted, and no Agatha Christies). And then we did something we hadn't done since our VW camper days—we read aloud to one another. *The Old Curiosity Shop* filled our flickering tent with Dickens's outrageous characters and dastardly intrigues. I read fragments of *The Prophet,* followed by romantic poems from *The Oxford Treasury* at appropriate intervals.

We slept for a while, then woke to the utter silence of the night. I cooked a small pasta dish in the early hours before dawn—fettuccine with double cream and smoked salmon sprinkled with fresh tarragon. We allowed ourselves one Perugina chocolate kiss each and two generous balloons of Rémy Martin.

Later, unused to the mattressed tent floor, I requested a massage and soon reciprocated. This led to more impassioned moments that reminded us why we'd married each other more than thirty years ago. Sort of honeymoon and first-date sensations all roiling together.

But perhaps our greatest pleasure was in talking. We played memory games to see how intensely we could recollect past experiences. We traded hopes and schemes and "what-if" scenarios. We remembered past homes and places we'd lived—our tiny cubist cottage in a remote Canary Island village; our cavelike Yorkshire Dales farm rented from the man who invented "Blue Wensleydale" cheese; our fancy apartment in Tehran when we worked for the Shah of Iran; our camper-homes both in southern Italy and for weeks exploring the wild places of Oregon's northern coast. We planned new adventures on a big, worn map of the world—a Sahara crossing, Inner Mongolia, a trek in Thailand's Golden Triangle, a journey to the lost Atlantis of the Azores, a beach-bum life in Goa for a few weeks, a trip behind the Himalayas to hidden Ladakh.

We slept again, and then we cooked together—crazy creations in puff pastry; tiny truffle quiches; English scones (more like real teeth-smashing "rock buns"); rolled phyllo things; liqueur-based dressings for watercress, endive and grape salads; a sinfully rich zabaglione. We even invented a rather unusual fruit punch crammed with fresh pineapple, mango slices, and passion fruit and called it the CCC—the Caribbean Compensation Concoction.

ZZ Top and old Chuck Berry tapes would wake us from lethargy, shaking the cottony pyramid of our tent; James Taylor and Jim Croce provided quieter interludes. We even rediscovered the tingle of rough-edged truths in early Bob Dylan songs. And then came the giant symphonies. We listened to all Beethoven's nine in a marathon session broken by reading, more reminiscing, and charcoal sketches of one another done by candlelight. We enjoyed a "Mostly Mozart" concert after a particularly intriguing luncheon of wafer-thin filet mignon slices barely warmed in a port and orange-zest sauce with sautéed mixed mushrooms and saffron couscous.

We got crazier as the weekend progressed. We wrote two short stories together and a few fragments of poems; we invented an odd board game; we designed our "perfect house" using favorite features of the thirty-odd different places we'd lived in since our marriage. We even plugged the phone back in for a while and made loving phone calls (from inside the tent) to people we missed and felt we'd overlooked.

Then somewhere in the middle of Sunday we decided to forget Monday: our WWW was too precious and enduring an experience to be terminated by the clock. So we made brief calls, canceled things and gave ourselves the gift of time.

We were on a soaring high, roller-coasting through emotions, finding new facets of each other. We created menus for future houseguests; we designed ridiculous furniture (a diamond-shaped dinner set; new ways to display books); we dreamed up four new businesses. We even wrote two songs, using my old, battered guitar for inspiration.

And as Monday merged into Tuesday, our WWW slowly wound down by itself, without anticlimaxes or withdrawal pains. We were satiated—gastronomically, emotionally, spiritually.

So we wrapped up the remnants of cheeses and pâtés, replaced the cushions, lowered the tent, tugged the mattress back to the bedroom. But we kept the lights low, the candles glowing and toasted one another with one last glass of Tattinger—or rather, not *one*-another, but *all* the others we'd discovered and rediscovered in each of us, during this most wonderful of wacky weekends.

PUB PEARLS

All Used Up

"When I die I want nothing left—absolutely nothing! Zilch! Nada!—I want everything used up, maxed out! If there's any money around I want it all handed out and used for somethin' good. I want m'heart full to the brim, busting—with all the good stuff, and I want my legs and knees gone after too much fun in crazy places, doing crazy things, my arteries clogged with years of glorious excess and my brain bustin' with the memories of explorings, experiments, discoverings—all the magic of living, so crammed full there's no room for anything more—'cept gettin' excited about the next big journey—the biggest trip of all...."

"Jeez, Harry—and I'm gettin' all worried 'bout a bit of arthritis in m' fingers."

Finding My Kami

The deity is instantly recognizable.

When I first came to Japan I knew very little about Shinto, or as some call it, "the ancient religion of nature." In fact, for some reason I'd never thought of the Japanese as being particularly religious. Of course I knew there were plenty of Buddhist temples, some very famous and exotic ones, especially those in Nikko, Tokyo, and Kyoto. I'd also heard that Zen was highly regarded in Japan, but still I assumed that, as in many Western nations, those religious beliefs had been nudged to the sidelines by the sheer preponderance of materialism and all the illusionary securities of newfound affluence.

So it came as something of a surprise when I wandered the countryside, deep in the mountainous heart of Japan, in the tight forested valleys with their ancient villages and tiny rice fields and bamboo groves and tumbling streams, to find Shinto shrines everywhere, marking a pantheon of sacred spots. They were often hidden away in deep woods on hills or mountains, by the side of fast-flowing rivers valued for their fish, or overlooking the tiny fields of rice, taro, corn, and onions. They were a ubiquitous feature of the landscape. As with Aboriginal

THE SHINTO GROVE · RICE FIELDS · NOBEOKA

Dreamtime sacred sites in Australia, which fill even the most featureless of bush-landscapes, these Shinto shrines reflect a deep Japanese respect and even awe for the manifestations of nature and the sacred spirits within.

Invariably the entrance to each Shinto shrine is marked by a torii gate, with its traditional upturned lintel set on two slightly splayed columns. Then in the compound beyond are usually two separate buildings—the *haiden,* or small worship room and the even smaller *honden,* home of the local nature spirit or the *kami,* and reached by half a dozen steep steps up from the rear of the *haiden.* The two are usually linked by a protective tiled roof. Adornments such as the straw ropes, or *shimenawa,* define sacred places and often encircle boulders and trees and smaller shrines. Sometimes the ropes are old and plain, frayed a little and fatter in the middle than at the two ends. Sometimes they're festooned with jagged folded paper strips called *gohe* that blow entrancingly in breezes and are meant to entice the occasionally wandering *kami* spirit back to its home in the *honden.*

It's all very ritualized but also enticingly simple. The *haiden* entrance is sometimes a mass of elaborately carved wooden dragons, elephant heads, lions, and other exotic, unearthly creatures or sometimes not, depending on the wealth of the village and the importance of the *kami.* The whole structure is usually of wood, unpolished and sometimes a little termite-ridden, and rests on large round rocks.

Shinto shrines are invariably silent. Even if one is located in the center of a village, when you climb the hill or enter the grove of trees to visit the shrine, the outside world seems to gently fade away and you find yourself alone, surrounded by rope-adorned boulders and trees, far from the distractions of everyday life. And if you pause and sit awhile and let the place ease into your consciousness, you begin to sense that you are surrounded by the most primitive and powerful of forces— those of earth, food sources, water, and trees for shelter, warmth, and the building of homes—all the basics of survival in an ancient world and all wrapped in timeless legends and myths that bound and still bind Japan together as a nation and set it apart from the rest of the world.

And that is how you feel in one of the shrines—separate from the world. And I had learned from a friend something of the mouth- and face-washing rituals normally performed here at the stone basin *(chzuya),* followed by the making of a modest offering, the bell-ringing, bowing, hand-clapping (to attract the attention of the *kami*) and a silent prayer or wish before bowing again and moving slowly backward from the shrine. And although I knew all this, I usually preferred to leave the rituals to the true believers and just enjoy the sanctity and silence of the grove, or stream, or hilltop.

But on one of my first visits I had a little surprise awaiting me. I was alone and had found this relatively modest, unadorned shrine hidden up a narrow trail in a magnificent grove of cryptomeria fir trees deep in a mountain gorge. The place was so silent I felt guilty making the slightest noise so I tiptoed around the site and finally found a boulder (non-sacred, no *shimenawa* rope around it) to sit on and sketch the structure and try to capture something of the utter peace of the place.

After half an hour or so I was quite pleased with the sketch and was preparing to leave when I had the oddest sensation. I felt as if an invisible hand was gently, but firmly, pushing me toward the *haiden*—the worship room. I didn't feel scared. In fact it seemed almost natural, as if some part of me had already anticipated it.

So I allowed myself to be led up the steps under the *shimenawa* rope and the bells where I removed my shoes, pushed the delicate, rice-paper-panelled doors of the *haiden* apart and entered a bare, dark room, unadorned, undecorated—just wooden walls, a creaky wooden floor (not even any straw tatami mats), and a small raised dais with a few offerings of half-filled sake bottles, incense, and candles. There was no fancy altar, no statuary, no chalices or tapestries or gilded riches or lavish statues. There was nothing at all, really, except the silence.

And the pushing continued, still gentle but insistent. But now I was really reluctant. I was being urged up onto the dais, through another set of sliding doors, and then outside the *haiden* and up the narrow steep steps to the *honden,* home of the *kami,* the god of this little corner of the world.

I was a little nervous. I had never even thought of approaching the *honden* before. It was strictly off-limits, or so I'd been led to believe. And it was a sealed structure anyhow—no windows, no peepholes, only a small door at the front, invariably locked. You were not meant to enter the *kami*'s domain, merely sense its presence and power.

I wanted to turn back but then something else happened. I knew in my mind and throughout my whole body that I was welcome here. I sensed I was not intruding. There was something I was being urged to see. But I had no idea what. I was not even sure what form the *kami* took—maybe a hideous sculptured creature like some of the Buddhist spirits beloved by Indonesian wood-carvers, with fangs and claws and bulging eyeballs and a fistful of human effigies being squeezed to excruciating death (admittedly, you see more of those in other Asian countries than Japan, but still...). In fact, I had never really thought of the *kami* as any *thing* at all but rather the spirit or essence of a place, and thus invisible.

The door to the *honden* had a padlock on it but, oddly, it was unlocked. I still wanted to go back. That's quite far enough, too far in fact, yelled one of my less courageous selves. I knew him well and I've labeled him Thomas in the past—the doubter, the coward, the cringer—and usually just calling his name is enough to discourage his antics.

Someone in me did say "get lost," and immediately he vanished and a feeling of calm fell on me like a thick, warm blanket. I saw my right hand stretching out to slide the door open very slowly. It was dark and musty inside although a little light trickled in through cracks in the old wooden walls. It was small too, barely five feet by five feet square. I eased forward. My head was now inside the *honden* and the musty smell was intense but tinged with the sweet aroma of incense, long since burned, but still lingering in the walls and wooden floor of the tiny space.

The calm was still with me so I sat on the top step and continued peering in until my eyes adjusted to the darkness. Then I noticed a *honden* in miniature with its own small raised dais, this time devoid of offerings. There was nothing else in the room. No startling statue, or blast of flame, or grotesque poison-spitting horror-creatures. There was quite simply—nothing.

And then there was something.

Above the dais, barely visible at first, mildewed with age, cracked and streaked with dust and cobwebs, was a mirror. Just a mirror. Nothing more. And staring back at me from the mirror, with a look of great surprise on its face, was not a *kami* at all.

It was just me.

And then I smiled and began to understand…

The longest journey is the journey inwards.
—DAG HAMMARSKJÖLD

The "Why" of the Wilderness

*The destination of all our wanderings becomes
clear through a surprising, but obvious, connection.*

Mantras come in curious guises.

"...bugga-loo, bugga-loo, bugga-loo..."

Certainly the hiker's rhythmic recitation captured something of the stolid, plodding, swamp-sodden thump and squelch of this seemingly endless bog-trotter trek. Invariably in fogbound solitude, I was lumbering alone across the vast purple wastes of heather, stunted bracken, needle-spiked tussocks of marsh grass and pernicious peat bogs—all the indigenous vegetation of the great North Yorkshire Moors of England—and coming to the end of one of the most arduous hikes I'd ever undertaken.

"Hi," I said to this blond-haired, backpack-laden giant whose undulating bulk I'd seen ahead of me for most of the cloud-shrouded, mizzly (splendidly descriptive Yorkshire dialect for the all-to-familiar mix of mist and drizzle) morning.

He turned reluctantly, still reciting his puffy mantra: "...bugga-loo, bugga—Oh, hello."

I detected a flicker of an accent, possibly German. "Novel use of the vernacular," I said, although I don't know why. Conversations, especially with a foreigner, are not always easy in the wilderness. You tend to become lost in your own miasma and metronome of walking rhythms as you—in my case a slightly corporeally challenged fellow—enjoy the rare luxury of aloneness and slowly heave your pack along the 190 or so miles of this famous hike across some of the wildest and most spectacular swaths of country in the whole of England.

The Coast-to-Coast Walk, one of Britain's best-loved of its many long-distance footpaths, wiggles its way pretty much due west to east (the best way to go, with the weather at your back) from the Irish Sea and the soaring 300-foot-high cliffs of St. Bees Head on Cumbria's western coast, through and sometimes over the very tops of the soaring crags of the Lake District National Park. Then it moves on into the treeless limestone fells across the most challenging northern sector of the Yorkshire Dales National Park, and finally across the high, heathered, wind-scoured domes of the North Yorkshire Moors National Park, to end in one of Britain's most delightful little North Sea communities, Robin Hood's Bay.

But back to my fellow hiker. He was obviously a little perplexed by my rather silly remark and paused in mid-stride. "Plis. What is zis *verna...*?"

"Vernacular," I offered, always ready to help out a fellow bog-trotter.

"Yes. What is zis word?"

"Oh, y'know, those good old Anglo-Saxon expressions you're using like a mantra when you walk." He looked at me.

Another perplexed pause. This is not a good start, I thought. Mantra, mantra, what's another word for *mantra?* Oh boy, the heck with it. Time for a break.

Two Blackface sheep watched our curious parting. I fell back on my pack and let everything go limp. I was bushed, tottering with tiredness. This was day twelve of the walk. I'd actually hoped to do it in ten as is the norm with fit hikers but decided, after a particularly grueling stretch over Nine Standards Rigg in the Dales, to ease up and dump my too-rigid itinerary. I was traveling "flex" as some call it, with my own tiny tent and sleeping bag so I didn't have to stick with some pre-booked sequence of B&Bs like so many Coast-to-Coasters.

I was just letting my eyelids droop for a brief nap when, from way ahead, I heard a yell. I looked up and there was my blond giant again, waving like a madman from the crest of the moor. Was there a problem? Was he hurt? I was tempted to just wave back and nod off, but didn't. Instead I hastily gathered up my pack and half-stumbled along the narrow turf path until I joined him, panting like a pig in heat.

"There," he said, pointing to the east. "Look!"

And it truly was a sight for sore, or in my particular case, sleepy eyes. The moors dropped away in one great purple plunge to the broad, emerald-green bowl of Eskdale, carved from soft shale bedrock more than 150 million years ago, laced with tiny fields and neat hedgerows and bosky copses and sheep-strewn meadows and a river and the spires of churches and smoke curls from farms and cottages and—way in the hazy mists—the dusky-blue infinities of the North Sea. "This is the epitome of the whole journey!" I gushed, and immediately wished I hadn't. Why this sudden indulgence in gaudy words? There was the inevitable pause.

"Plis. What is zis *epit....*"

This is so typical of me. Prattling on about the end of the journey when I should be describing the start and the middle. So—as they say—let's begin at the beginning.

I dipped my hiking boots, as is the custom, in the churlish surf of the Irish Sea at St. Bees, turned my back on this little coastal town of no particular charm, and began an immediate climb up the edge of the soaring red sandstone cliffs. Kittiwakes, fulmars, and scores of those always-frantic little puffins whirled around me.

The weather was, as English weather often tends to be, pallidly monochromatic with flaccid suggestions of showers. And barely had I begun to plant one boot in front of the other than I got my first attack of the "why bothers"—why am I about to spend my hard-won vacation time slogging my way across 190 miles of mountains and moors when I could be...well, you know the feeling. And I wondered that same "why" many times on this arduous odyssey. In fact it became something of a grail-like search for a clear answer. Thoreau once wrote: "True and sincere traveling is no pastime but it is as serious as the grave...and it requires a long probation to be broken into." I'm not sure any of us ever actually gets beyond the probation phase—traveling, particularly a long and lonely hike, is such a powerful catalyst of self-exploration. And if the self is potentially infinite in its capacity for revelation then...well, you get the point.

But I decided philosophical retrospection would not be prominent on my agenda for that first morning. There was hiking to be done. And what remarkable hiking it was for those few days across the Lake District, starting off pleasantly enough up pastoral valleys, alongside the River Ehen, with Ennerdale Water—my first lake—close by, and then becoming progressively more challenging as the fells closed in and the narrow path began its climb through the village of Dent with vistas of the great summits—Skiddaw, High Stile, Pillar, and Scafell Pike—way ahead.

I was lucky. The fickle fall weather suddenly brightened. Sunlight glinted like quicksilver on the chittering streams and crisp breezes were filled with the aromas of cut hay. A great blue sky dome, dotted with tiny clouds dainty as duck down, calmed the drama of the peaks. They looked benevolent, accessible, almost too easy.

And then I was not so lucky. In typical Lakeland fashion and with virtually no warning, a cold front moved in off the Irish Sea, blocking out vistas of the Isle of Man to the west and transforming this scene of pastoral harmony into a murky squodge—a pea-soup-green miasma of slanting rain, winds that ripped at my parka jacket like ravenous rat packs, and a great sponge pudding of gray cloud that obliterated not only the majestic hills but almost everything ahead except for the sinuous path itself, rapidly being transformed into a mud mire with boggy patches marked (a useful warning) by tiny clusters of bog asphodel.

I took shelter in a thick copse by the path, humbled by nature's caprices, and unburdened myself of a backpack which already I knew was far too overloaded for the journey (and that was after three radical, throw-everything repackings). At first all I could hear was the thud and splatter of rain and the rumbles of distant thunder. And then came voices. Two fellow hikers emerged out of the mess, fresh-paced and chirpily high-spirited. They spotted me lurking in the bushes.

"Nice day," shouted one through the din.

"For ducks!" added his companion.

And then they were gone. So much for the famed Coast-to-Coast camaraderie! I mooched on for another few miles along an increasingly gooey path and then, thankful I didn't have to struggle on to honor a B&B booking, made a camp of sorts in another copse in Nannycatch Gate, halfheartedly cooked up one of those anonymous camp-soup packets on my propane stove, and decided to sleep early...

...and rise early. Just after a glorious dawn chorus, although, when I threw back the tent flaps, I wondered what all the gleeful twittering had been about. Everything was still gray. Not even a promising gray with dabs and freckles of sun glints. Just a lousy, corpse-colored gray.

But as I approached the summit of High Crag, everything changed. The muck of the morning dissipated and the air once again became diamond sharp and the sun scalding hot beneath, believe it or not, another perfect blue sky. It was the last of the bad weather for a few days and I walked and sang and supped at mountain streams, camped on the cusp of idyllic vista points, and gazed at the glorious panoramas as they unfolded—the gentle curl of Crummock Water, the brittle, moss-layered out-croppings of Haystacks, the tiny jewel of Innominate Tarn and the deep, inviting waters of Buttermere, and Milton's phrase "heaven on earth" is most appropriate.

Heaven, alas, did not endure as poor little Grasmere appeared, an attractive slate-stone village smothered in weekend tourists and littered with trinket shops, tearooms, bacon-buttie places (don't ask), and chips-with-everything pubs. I left quickly and chose the "hard option" of the Walk over the crags of 3,118-foot-high Helvellyn and along the notorious knife-blade of Striding Edge (all edge and little striding, more like shuffling on the lip of an abyss). I'd done this section eons ago as a school kid with boundless energy determined to prove my manhood, or something like that. Now I was that man and the boundless energy seemed to have been dissipated a little by the years. However, I made it (asking the eternal "why bother" all along)

and was rewarded by more panoramas of the whole of Lakeland and an easy descent into quiet Patterdale where I gave myself a day off to prepare for the next set of challenges.

A couple of days later I rolled into Kirkby Stephen, a funky pre-Norman market town at the western edge of the Yorkshire Dales complete with sheep auctions (scores of flat-capped farmers in worn tweed jackets, two bawling auctioneers and hundreds of terrified sheep), a welcome array of pubs and inns, great fish 'n' chip shops, and hikers and bikers galore.

"Oh yeah, there's quite a few of us do t' biking version of t' Walk," said Sam Taylor from Manchester. "There's horse-riding and driving versions too—'England's Wildest Drive,' they call it. All kinda ways, all kinda people. Some doin' it for charity, tha's become a big thing now. Some competin' or doin' it for a bet. But most of 'em, well, they do it for 'emselves a reckon', just for t' hell of it. I suppose it's a way of pushin' yerself a bit...." He was certainly right there. The Walk was pushing me way beyond the familiar boundaries of pain and

weariness, but it was also opening up fresh dimensions of determination and exhilaration.

Then suddenly I was in the Yorkshire Dales, one of my favorite parts of northern England, and full of boyhood memories of hikes and camps and even a couple of adolescent romantic interludes. This muscular part of the Pennine Range, which runs like a buckled spine up through the north of England into Scotland, is a bold mountain and moor region cut by deep, green valleys (dales), and spiderwebbed with drystone walls enclosing tiny pastures and meadows. It presents an enduring portrait of sweeping, desolate splendor and wild upland loneliness and is rich with the weft and woof of northern history sagas from the Ice Age hunters to the Celts, Vikings, Normans and the great eleventh- to sixteenth-century monastic heritage. Each has left its distinct imprint on the quaintly huddled hamlets, wind-scoured fells, the somnolent stepped profiles of the great limestone mountains and the sheep-sprinkled coziness of the deep dales.

The weather did not greet me as a welcome homecomer, however, and turned churlish again as I slurped my way on the fringes of more peat bogs, past the Nine Standards Rigg Cairns in a rip-your-knickers-off rainstorm, and became utterly lost for hours in a trackless world of thick white fog and ankle-snapping rocks. I met another me here briefly—an unwelcome me that dreads a miserable unsung demise in a howling wilderness. Finally, through sheer stubborness (my compass skills atrophied), I almost tumbled headlong down into the deep ravine of Boggle Hole, cut by the embryonic River Swale, and arrived exactly where I'd intended, at the home of Doreen Whitehead in Keld.

Doreen is a large, loquacious lady with a broad Dales accent who literally wrote the book on the Walk, at least in terms of listing the scores of B&Bs along the route in her little publication. "She's saved many of us from frigid wet nights out on t' moors," one grateful hiker told me.

For years Doreen has seen the walkers pass through her clustered stone-built village, with its thick mullion windows and rich in Viking associations dating to the tenth century when all this region was occupied by those fierce Scandinavian invaders. She loves to chat and enjoys a little name-dropping. "Prince Charles likes it 'ere—loves me chocolate cake too! He came to visit us not long back. He seemed a different person up in these parts, very natural. Very nice young man."

Farther down, the Swale matures into broad sinuous curls as the valley widens and becomes softer, leaving the great out-croppings and scarps of eroded limestone behind.

After a welcome pub-pause with a motley bunch of farmers and hikers at the Black Bull in Reeth, one of Swaledale's most beautiful villages, sprawled languorously around a huge green, I decided it was time once again to give myself the gift of time. And thanks to the charms of nearby tenth-century

Richmond, one of England's finest "undiscovered gems," I was enticed into the self-indulgent, Falstaffian world of ancient inns with downy beds, huge Yorkshire breakfasts (bacon, black pudding, sausage, fried eggs, mushrooms, tomatoes, beans, fried bread); big dinners of pork pies and mushy peas, steak and kidney pudding, sticky toffee sponge, sherry trifle, spotted dick and the like; and all the now-unfamiliar comforts of home. This tightly packed, history-thick town, with its castle set on towering cliffs above the Swale, cobbled market square, narrow streets and alleys cascading down impossibly steep gradients, felt like a major metropolis after all the vast empty spaces behind me.

But in a couple of days it was back to the tromp and tent and backpack bruises and an increasingly painful ailment known as "shin splints," which makes your lower legs feel to be on fire or suffering from a hearty dowsing in strong acid. My goal now was just to get there—to complete the hike and try to figure out all the "why bothers" later on.

The walk entered a rather dull phase, a twenty-mile crossing of the pancake-flat fields of the Vale of Mowbray, before finally arriving in the village of Osmotherley, at the base of my final challenge—the darkly brooding, purple wastes of the Cleveland Hills and the North Yorkshire Moors.

And quite a challenge it was. I almost gave up on that first night, high up on the aptly named plateau of Cold Moor among infinite deserts of ankle-snaring heather and yet more bogs, as a storm moved in and stayed all through the dark hours, thrashing my tiny tent and shrieking at times like covens of cruel witches and sending shivers of almost primordial panic down my spine. And then something very odd happened. A voice—a deep voice inside me—said very clearly and patiently, "David— you're safe—you're already way past this." That was all. And then the voice faded but left me feeling calm and at peace.

Then things improved once again and for two days I seemed to float across the purple heights sprinkled with ancient moorland crosses, peering down the Shangri-La-like valleys of Farndale and Rosedale, dining at the Lion Inn, perched on the highest part of the moors and one of the Walk's most popular stop-offs (renowned particularly for its gargantuan breakfasts), and feeling that I might actually be able to complete my odyssey intact and indelibly stamped with its power and beauty.

And so it was that in the company of my mantra-mumbling German companion I crested that last long stretch of moor, and the vast horizons of the North Sea, deep blue against a suddenly golden sky, were spread before me. My destination was finally within reach.

One of my favorite travel writers, Jonathan Raban, suggests that "travel is inherently a plotless, disordered, chaotic affair...it may take a year or more to see there was any point to the thing at all."

And after fourteen days of blisters on top of blisters, bruises and bloodied knees, gnarly leg cramps, and a heart that threatened to finally stop pumping at the next sign of another hill—I was convinced that the whole thing was indeed a very "chaotic affair."

But I was lucky. It didn't take a year to see there was any point to the thing at all. It actually all came together as easily and deliciously as the warm beer and British "crisps" down in a pub at Robin Hood's Bay.

It was late in the day when I arrived at this beloved endpoint of the walk, once notorious for its smugglers and now best known as a picturesque haven of history. The cliff suddenly vanished into a cleft packed higgledy-piggledy tight with tiny bronze-colored stone houses topped with red pantile roofs, clustered limpetlike along a vertiginous lane wriggling down to a rock-bound beach. Once again, I seemed to be the only walker around but I obeyed the time-honored ritual, doused my boots in the frothy surf of the North Sea, and then collapsed in the tiny bar of The Dolphin to sup a celebratory pint of amber ale with the cheery landlord, David Mason.

David, it turned out, was an old master of the Walk. "Four times—last one were not long back for a charity do."

"Why so many times?" I asked and got one of those typically elusive Yorkshire responses.

"Well—it were handy I suppose. Right on t' doorstep, like."

I persisted. "C'mon David, what's the real reason?"

David paused, his perpetual grin faded into something a little more serious. "Well, it made me appreciate m'own company, I suppose." He paused again, sipped his beer slowly, and then added the clincher: "You feel a real explorer again for a while. You grow. You come home a bigger person than you thought you were."

And there it was. That was it in all its simplicity. That was *precisely* the key to the whole experience for this "why bother" walker who'd left St. Bees a couple of weeks back and had faced—albeit reluctantly at times—a few more challenges than he'd expected. And then it suddenly came to me. That voice I'd heard so clearly in my head on that wild moorland night? It was my late father's voice. No doubt about it. It was his intonation and his gentle wisdom. It was *him*...

Outside I could hear the evening surf walloping the rocks and hissing around the tidewrack and wondered if this walking thing might start to become a little addictive. I find I like coming home a little larger, shaking the kaleidoscope of my life, adding (and occasionally discarding) a newly discovered self or two, and most wonderful of all on this adventure, finding my father again. Deep inside me.

Ode to Onions

We are all onions...
—crisp yet juicy
—pungent yet perfumed
—sharp yet sweet
—round yet full of edges
—tough-skinned yet soft and white within
—whole yet infinitely fragmented
    and layered
    and layered
    and layered
    and layered
Almost
    to total
        transparency

The Wildest Places of All

A friend had a plane, a tiny Piper Cherokee, forever tied down at a runway, too far out of town for casual jaunts. He dreamed of great journeys—an Atlantic crossing via Newfoundland and the Azores; a Pacific odyssey full of touchdowns on deserted islands; a world circumnavigation with stops in all the forgotten places. But the plane just sat there, full of tantalizing possibilities, draped in dreams.

What a splendid idea, to bid farewell to the concrete calamities and the tawdry aesthetics of the earthbound, to leave the earth for a while and touch the wild places inside once again, to lift up, out, and off, leaping into infinities.

So we did.

And there, beneath the careful man clogged by schedules and mind-bound by meetings, was the spirit of the boy, brimming with fantasies, clutching the cirrus tails, reaching out to touch new possibilities.

A small plane is pure magic. The runway skims by, the engine screaming in anticipation, the nose lifts, the seat springs groan and creak as your body weight doubles in that first thrust of flight, and—you're off. The ground drops away, becoming a rinky-dink, toy-town picture book of dollhouses and Matchbox cars and spongy trees and tiny white-spired churches.

The world is all yours. You can go anywhere, do anything, turn left, turn right, fly in circles, climb, dive, do a somersault, loop-a-loop if you must, play peekaboo with clouds, chase a rainbow, tease a thunderhead, skim the spuming surf, kiss a mountain top, make the long grasses wave like silky hair, roll your wings at a farmer in his field, bombard the cumulus galleons with their wind-ripped sails. Your spirit soars with the plane; you feel light as duck down, free as a feather. And you remember, you know again, just how precious and perfect life and being alive can be. The high of the whole. The best high of all. Because it's true.

Look up and it's a pure Mediterranean-blue dome, arching over to a golden haze. Look down and the patterns intermingle: the patchwork patterns of fields, a random quilt of greens and golds and ochres; the pocket-comb geometrics and curlicues of plowed furrows; the silver-flashed streams; the baroque tangles of woods and copses on humping hills; the sprinkle of villages along a tattered coastline ribboned with white surf. Gone are the gas stations and the hype strips of neon-decked motels and junk-food stands and auto showrooms and traffic lights and do-this-do-that signs and billboards and all the gaudy excess of street-bound life.

This was a new world up here, fresh, bright, traffic free—and for a moment, all mine! I wanted to shout down to farmers and tell them how beautiful their fields looked—bold abstract masterpieces of color and form that could grace the walls of any gallery. I saw lovely things: a single fishing boat with the shadow of a galleon, apexed in a flat pyramid of cut ocean; the fluid lines of submerged reefs, receding in filigreed layers from turquoise to the deepest of royal blues; moonscapes of gravel pits and quarries concealing pools of clear green water; the silty delicacy of estuaries edged by curled traceries of emerald marshes; Frankenthaler earth patterns of water absorption in fields of new wheat. It was an aesthetic unfamiliar to me. A world of fresh beauty, of juxtapositions of form, color, and texture I'd never imagined before.

Evening eased in slowly and seemed to last forever. As the sun slid down into its scarlet haze, we rose up to watch the shadows scamper across the rolling land. A modest line of trees following a winding country road cast quarter-mile-long shadows, purpling the furrows. Little hillocks produced mountain-sized echoes of themselves across the fields. Even a tiny white farm and a cluster of barns and outbuildings became a Versailles shadow, suggesting towers, turrets, and elegant cornices. Cows were giraffes; a tiny red truck became a triple-decker bus; a man heading for home across a bronze field was a stick-legged giant.

And when the night came, it came with grace through the drowsy half-dark, in a slow canopy of velvety purple, sprinkled with stars. The west gave up its glow with reluctance and the night allowed a dignified retreat. An equitable ritual, well rehearsed over the eons. And we watched the gentleness of it all, floating easily in the evening air, not wanting to leave, reluctant to face the disordered scramble of earthly matters. So we flew on, abandoning ideas for a touchdown somewhere in the flatlands below us. Food and flight plans, taxis, motels, and beds could all wait. The night invited us to stay and we accepted, watching it flow in, filling the lower places, rising up the flanks of the ranges, leaving little islets of light on the high tops for a while until they too were submerged in the deepening purple tide as we floated on into the mysteries of the dark.

Up here, apart from it all, indivisible, you sense greater perceptions—hierarchies of knowingness just beyond the next truth. Like the paradox of particle physics, never quite getting there, merely seeing deeper and deeper, space beyond space into the inner universe with its constellations of quarks (strange, charmed, and all those other multicolored entities), mesons, gluons, neutrinos, gravitons (and even antigravitons), matching the complexity and scale of the outer universe itself. An equilibrium of endlessness.

Up here, floating, you see it all quite clearly. The clamor of experiences, the search for other selves tantalizingly out of reach, even beyond, for the moment, the bounds of comprehension. Seeking the mind of the Creator in the fragmentary illusions of everyday life, playing with his possibilities, cracking open the creaky walls of knowledge and flying out into pure beingness.

I wished it would all last forever. But of course, it didn't, and finally we were back to the swelling hills of home, bosky with copses and stringy streams and things with associations, leaving all the wild places behind for a while.

But happy with one thought.

That the wildest places of all are our own infinite array of selves, deep within, and there's no end to the exploration and enjoyment of their mysteries and magic.

And that is sufficient.

For the moment....

ABOUT THE AUTHOR

A native of Yorkshire, England, David Yeadon has worked as an author, illustrator, journalist, and photographer for more than twenty-five years. An author of more than twenty travel books, Yeadon has specialized in hidden corner and back road exploration. In *The Back of Beyond: Travels to the Wild Places of the Earth*, and its sequel, *Lost Worlds: Exploring the Earth's Remote Places*, he describes his worldwide search for the hidden, the remote, the unusual, and the exotic. He is also a regular travel correspondent for *National Geographic, National Geographic Traveler, The Washington Post, The New York Times,* and many other major travel magazines, with over 200 published features since 1985. In 1993, he received the Society of American Travel Writers (SATW) Lowell Thomas Gold and Silver Medals for best travel book and best foreign travel feature. Currently, he writes the "Hidden America" column for *National Geographic Traveler* and is completing a National Geographic book on *The World's Secret Places.* In between travel odysseys he lives with his wife, Anne, in Japan, where she is a Professor in Vision Rehabilitation, and also in a Hudson Valley lakeside house, just far enough north of Manhattan to preserve soul and sanity.

——— and the journeys continue.....